William Bement Lent

Across the Country of the Little King

A trip through Spain

William Bement Lent

Across the Country of the Little King
A trip through Spain

ISBN/EAN: 9783743402119

Manufactured in Europe, USA, Canada, Australia, Japa

Cover: Foto ©Andreas Hilbeck / pixelio.de

Manufactured and distributed by brebook publishing software (www.brebook.com)

William Bement Lent

Across the Country of the Little King

CONTENTS.

	PAGE
Introductory: Dei Gratia Alphonso XIII	1
The Gate by which we Entered—Gibraltar No. 1	10
The Gate by which we Entered—Gibraltar No. 2	18
An Outlying Post—Tangier	26
Our First Spanish Town—Ronda	40
A Moorish Legacy—The Alhambra No. 1	51
A Moorish Legacy—The Alhambra No. 2	61
A Moorish Legacy—The Alhambra No. 3	69
Some Granadian Fragments—Granada	79
The Oven of Spain—Seville No. 1	89
The Oven of Spain—Seville No. 2	98
Cæsar and Pilate—Seville	106
Here and There in Seville	115
Corpus Christi in Seville	124
With Murillo in Seville	135
The Pride of Cordova	144
Golden Hours in Cordova and Aranjuez	154
The Crown of Spain—Toledo	164
The Largest Village in Spain—Madrid	176
The Eighth Wonder of the World—The Escorial	187
A Spanish University Town—Salamanca	198
The City of the Cid—Burgos	208
By Biscay's Shore—San Sebastian, etc	217
The Birthplace of a Devotee	226
Au Revoir	234

LIST OF ILLUSTRATIONS.

	PAGE
Alfonso XIII, King of Spain................Frontispiece	
The Queen Regent, The Little King, The Two Infantas	8
Gibraltar..	24
The Alhambra, Court of Lions	70
Garden of the Generalife, Granada...............	82
Seville, Cathedral and Giralda.....................	100
The Alcazar Gardens, Seville	131
The Mosque, Cordova................................	146
Cordova Cathedral, Court of Oranges............	151
Toledo Cathedral Choir.............................	167
Toledo, Cloister San Juan de los Reyes	171
Burgos Cathedral, The Nave	211

ACROSS THE COUNTRY OF THE LITTLE KING.

INTRODUCTORY.

DEI GRATIA, ALFONSO XIII.

Spain, with a magnificent territorial stretch from north to south of four hundred and sixty miles, a regal sweep from east to west of some five hundred and sixty more, a constellation of provinces, soft and melodious in nomenclature and strangely varied in character, with a history unusually opulent in startling episodes and thrilling reminiscences and a literature rich in poetic fancy and romantic suggestion, is nevertheless the country of a very little King, for a lad of scarce eleven summers holds by inheritance the traditional purple and carries the title of Alfonso XIII., although well-nigh overwhelmed with the name of Alfonso Leon Fernando Maria Jakob Isodor Pascual! While the happiest years, probably, of this royal life are passing, the Queen-Mother, as Regent, holds, with rare tact, ability and judgment, the silken reins of government and exercises the remnant of power left, by successive revolutions and radical political changes, to the ruling Sovereign.

The most interesting of the two figures, however, at present, is the Queen Regent, of whom it is said that "the Spaniards awoke after the death of the late King, to find a woman in the palace they had really never known before." She, who had been merely an ornamental but stainless figure in the brilliant and corrupt court of Alfonso XII. determined to hold the kingdom for her unborn son, and rose so courageously and ably to the situation, as to command almost universal admiration and respect. If current gossip is reliable, she is an attached and watchful Mother and a devoted, conscientious and hardworking Sovereign. After all, these older continental monarchical countries are not ripe for self-government. They do better for a generation or two with their accustomed governmental head, handicapped by the will of the people, crystallized in a constitution. The Republic was a failure because its immature leaders lacked the most important attribute of self-government,—

"the power to subordinate their personal inclinations to the permanent good." Even Castelar, sturdy Republican as he is, concedes that the Spaniards have all the liberty they are ready for, in the present form of government, and casts in his allegiance, while unwilling to accept any official position. Said an Englishwoman, while speaking of the radical and sweeping changes upon the chess-board of political Europe during the last half century, and the possibility of this spectre or any transformation entering into the proud stronghold of England's Empire, "Oh! *we* will always have a King or Queen if only for a *figurehead!*" Surely there is no more pathetic figurehead than the delicate, innocent little boy-King of Spain, Alfonso XIII., and one scarcely knows whether most to pity or congratulate. The awakening, everywhere more or less perceptible in the grand old kingdom, will give birth to problems, and life to conflicting elements that will require a well-balanced head and a mighty arm. The future, unless all the signs of the times are incorrect, means "business" to the little King and a life of unceasing toil and care. Curiosity, therefore, to see one who is likely, if life be prolonged, to be prominent in future history, is legitimate. True, it is only a child; but the boy is father of the man, and it is the coming King for weal or woe that all want to see. Fortunately abundant opportunity is given in Madrid, where he may frequently be seen by the palace windows overlooking the daily mounting of the guard or while driving, almost unattended, through the city streets; while at San Sebastian, where the Queen has a lovely villa by the sea, much of the rigid court etiquette seems less conspicuous, and the little fellow plays by the shore or disports in the water in plain sight, much as any happy child would do. With an allowance from the government of one million four hundred thousand dollars a year, the lad bids fair, when he reaches his majority, to be the richest sovereign in Europe. Yet common as a by-word is the oft repeated assertion, "Spain is bankrupt." Even to the passing tourist the country and people seem poor and paralyzed and fully a generation behind the rest of the continent. But the blessed railway has entered in, and there is no such innovator and awakener as the iron horse and the metal way. Spain, like Russia, seems under a spell; but some day this will be broken and the torpid, dormant life leap into progress and prosperity again. The question of what form of government it has, seems of less importance than the elevation and emancipation of the people through common education and religious freedom. If the little King lives the allotted three score years and ten, his reign will witness radical changes, and, let us hope, unbounded progress and development also. During our sojourn in Madrid, we whiled away very pleasantly a couple of hours in visiting the Queen's stables and repository of Royal carriages, etc.,—a display and array quite unlike and surpassing any other that we have seen save that at St. Petersburg. We were ushered at once into a long, low-ceiled room like a hall or corridor, some two hundred and fifty or three hundred feet in length, with brilliantly polished floors, and along the side walls and through the centre a continuous row of handsome glass cases, in which were displayed all the paraphernalia and trappings of State ceremonials, social functions, the chase and the national bull-fights. Gorgeous sets of red and black and russet gold-mounted harness, — magnificently ornamented saddles,—all the rich costumes of jockeys and liveries for coachmen, footmen and outriders,—most elaborately trimmed outfits in yellow, blue, green and red gold-laced satins for the Royal bull-fights,—profusely embroidered suits and trappings for matadors and picadors, and all the sumptuous, showy and elaborate appointments for horses and carriages upon State occasions, succeeded one another in processional brilliancy and effect. Some cases were filled with pyramids of richest ostrich plumes in all colors, in colossal aigrettes used upon the horses' heads upon all State ceremonials. A replica of "Crazy Jane's" harness in lustreless black, most elaborately and beautifully pressed into ornamental designs, was the only sombre item in the glittering mass. We passed into a cloister and down to stable after stable in which, stalled upon either side of a central aisle, were carriage and saddle horses and a number of the prettiest little ponies. It was unsatisfactory, for out of the two to three hundred horses, not more than a half dozen were unblanketed. Fortunately two of the celebrated Aranjuez breed were being led out for exercise, and we had a fine view of the graceful cream-colored beauties. But the famous mules—the Royal steeds of black and cream colors—were not shown. Somehow, one could not help, in thought, comparing this sumptuous provision for the King's pets with the wretched housing of thousands of his faithful subjects, or wonder at the destructive fury of the mob, when revolution sets it free. Then we passed into an immense, barn-like structure in which, in a row all around, were a great variety of vehicles,—old-fashioned travelling coaches with trunks or boxes fitted and strapped to the top, tall drags, children's gigs and carriages, landaus, coupés and victorias by the dozen. In an adjoining building, equally barn-like, were the State coaches, some thirteen in all, gorgeous and showy with glitter of gilding, gleam of tortoise-shell, flash of ormolu and rich coloring of paintings. The body of one was of polished mahogany with ormolu decorations; another was of tortoise-shell; another, presented by Napoleon I., was a dazzling mass of exquisite ormolu. The most tasteful was that in which Alfonso II., the father of the little King, drove to his marriage service, with an elegant hammer-cloth, embroidered linings and side lamps surmounted by jewelled crowns. The spectre at the feast was that in which Queen Joanna, or "Crazy Jane," carried around the body of her husband wherever she went for forty-seven years, —a huge coach finished in dull jet and sombre cloth,—as repulsive as a hearse. Noticing in the large building some confusion and moving to and fro, which betokened preparations for something, we inquired the reason and were told "His Majesty, the King, would drive out in a half hour." We hurried over to the entrance of the Palace, for was not the little King one of the sights we had come so far to see?—and did it not become good plain Republicans, with a supposed contempt for that divinity which is commonly supposed to hedge about a King, to be first and foremost in the curious and waiting crowd? For fifteen minutes we stood in the shadow of the immense palace façade—facing a tall arched passage through the building to the great interior court, —the carriage standing in plain sight. Presently four uniformed, mounted guards came jauntily out and took positions upon one side, where they stood like statues. Following, a moment later, was a plain, handsome, open landau—drawn by four sleek black mules, as glossy and shiny as satin, —"the King's own." Within sat a lady, so simply and quietly attired in a figured lawn or organdie and an ordinary "sun hat," that, at first glance, we thought her a governess or attendant. But the hundreds of photographs in the shop windows make one so familiar with her face that in a moment we saw it was the Queen Regent. Another day we saw her returning from some public ceremonial, richly and appropriately dressed, "every inch a queen." With

The Queen Regent,

    The Little King,

        The Two Infantas.

her were two little girls also very simply dressed, and a delicate, fair-haired boy, with a wide-brimmed leghorn straw hat, which he vainly tried to lift repeatedly from his head in acknowledgment of the salute of the onlookers. Small, frail and colorless, the posthumous son of a dissolute sire, we wondered if this little head, with the waving hair, would ever be made uneasy by the traditional wearing of the crown! In the decided resemblance to his august Mother lies the hope that in character and efficiency he may reflect her record rather than that of the late King. But, in view of the disturbed state, the poverty, the undeveloped condition of the whole country, financially, socially and politically, the future years of the little monarch bid fair to be so crowded with conflict, confusion and change, that this dear little fellow, passing so unconsciously in an open carriage for an afternoon drive, seemed, for the time being, the most pathetic and pitiful figure in the whole panorama of European sights and interests.

THE GATE BY WHICH WE ENTERED.

The admirable steamer service, inaugurated within the last few years, direct from New York to the various ports of the Mediterranean, has made Gibraltar, although an English military station, the gate by which a great multitude of tourists enter the country of the little King, thereby avoiding repetition of tedious miles of travel and rendering a trip through central Spain quite as feasible as any ordinary European route. Our approach to it, upon a lovely glowing May morning, from earliest waking until our feet at last pressed upon the English soil, was spectacular and dramatic in the extreme, being full of exciting interest and varied beauty of earth and sea and sky. It seemed like a grand moving panorama in which there was absolutely nothing to mar or regret. We awoke in Trafalgar Bay, whose shimmering waters were so calm, sunny and serene that the story of the naval engagement of October 21, 1805, sounded like a myth. We had fairly entered, when we reached the deck, "the gate of the narrow passage," as the Arabs call the Straits of Gibraltar, some thirty-five or forty miles in length and twelve miles in width at the narrowest point,—at Tarifa,—where the learned men contend that, at some remote period, the two continents were joined. We stood entranced with the gradually unfolding picture. Away off in a little nook, a dazzling mass of pearly white was pointed out as Tangier; some flashing walls and battlements told of Tarifa; upon one side the low lying, verdant, undulating coast of Spain, and upon the other the waving, tossing range of mysterious African mountains, with soft opalescent tints and exquisite shadows slumbering in every indentation. While watching, as for a coming morning, for the first glimpse of the mighty leonine rock of Gibraltar, one by my side joyfully said, "I see it! I see the Lion!" A plain woman, a stranger, near by, looking intently at the nearer shore, exclaimed, "Oh! where? where is there a lion? I do not see one!" In speechless wonder we saw the rest of the golden way against a glowing eastern sky all enveloped in glorious light,—nature's majestic, royal couchant Lion, its rocky sides touched with vegetation and gilded with patches of yellow gorse—lifting its head some fourteen hundred and thirty feet above the waves. The effect is most peculiar, for the great mass rises direct from the sea, and the environing land is so flat that, as some one has said, it looks like " a fragment of some shattered world dropped here by chance." It certainly does not appear as if it belonged there, and looks the apple of discord it has ever been. At seven o'clock we were within the bay, the anchor was dropped, and our voyage was ended! Those who were going on to Naples hurried ashore for a two hours' drive and inspection. But the blessed time had come when there was no need for us to hurry, when nothing was hounding us remorselessly along, and we could sit and leisurely enjoy the unique scene. Directly before us stood, with grim, defiant, self-conscious air, yet harmless look, the stately rock, with, far away upon its precipitous and steep sloping sides, lifted up above the shore, tiny structures like white dots upon its face — with great yellow patches of flowering gorse, the red flag of England dominating all, and at the base, quite Italian-like in appearance, a town of great barracks and habitations, with dashes of color here and there, of riotous tropical-like growth of tree and flower. We could have remained there for hours, so fascinating and tumultuous were the impressions, thoughts and emotions that crowded upon our minds. A multitude of lifelong day-dreams knocked to say good-bye, for reality had crowded them out and dissipated their soft glamour; like a confused harmony and psalm, the scriptural phrases of "The Rock" as a precious symbol and figure sounded in our ears; and all the while, tossed high in air like a great tidal wave with its summit ridge almost as thin as crest of mountain billow, rose the majestic mass. We wondered if we had not known it was pierced, and seamed, and tunnelled with all that modern military ingenuity and knowledge could suggest, and bristled along its whole length of three miles with some two thousand or more cannon, whether it would have seemed as defiant and challenging in expression. Yet a leonine contour, even in a placid landscape, always breathes of force and impresses with strength. We went ashore in a steam tender, and, as we stepped upon the wharf, were suddenly conscious that we had entered upon a fresh and novel existence. A swarm of dusky, swarthy athletes, workingmen and idlers, with here and there a Moor or Barbary Jew in picturesque drapings and colors, surrounded us. Demure and patient donkeys with huge panniers upon either side, loaded high with cutting of fresh grass so full of crimson vetch blossoms as to be most artistic and tasteful, women in queer wrappings and foldings, and a half dozen little two-seat phaetons with white curtains and the unmistakable English girl waiting at the market, added to the tone, color and character of the scene. We entered the arched gates of the city, and, much amused, walked along the principal street — " Waterport "—to the Hotel Royal. Such a grotesque mixture of signs and people! A huge poster, near which was a gorgeously attired Moor, affirmed unblushingly "Alcock's Porous Plaisters,—the best." As I was in the embrace of two, I felt like confirming it for the possible benefit of the Scythian and Greek, bond and free, crowd around us! An hour later, in one of the amusing little vehicles, we were off for a drive, calling first upon our Consul for an official request for a pass to visit the rock galleries and batteries, which we were then obliged to present at the Governor-General's residence for confirmation—formerly an ancient convent, enclosing two courts, one of which was laid out with profusely crowded flower-beds and tropical plants. To one side stretched out a lovely garden with luxuriant growth of palms, callas, tuberoses, pomegranates, hibiscus, tree heliotropes (six feet in height), larkspurs, marigolds, wallflowers, hollyhocks, marguerites, gorgeous pelargoniums, and geraniums, blood-red poppies, flowering pepper trees and fruit-laden orange trees, all in full blossom. The garden is an English addition. Oh! this flower-loving English people! how they make even the desert glad with wild riot of floral bloom and color! The air was heavy with the mingled perfume and the repose and quiet, like unto a rest that remaineth. Later, armed with the official permit, we drove by zigzag roads, passing comical little streets of steps, and many windows and terraces just overflowing with flowers, to high upon the mountain side, to visit the galleries shown to ordinary visitors. While waiting upon an open plateau for a guide, we looked, through the great straggling branches of sycamore trees, in gardens below—way down upon quiet blue waters with idle ships—fishing-boats and winged lateen sails, upon a lovely painted ocean and on to snatches of the green Spanish hills. The ancient sycamores were most quaint and picturesque—with so many long, spread-out branches that seemed to invite one to be seated, that we readily understood why "Zaccheus he did climb a tree" to see the Master pass. A more delightful tiny Meissonier could not be imagined than the sight through these branches upon the little shadow-flecked, flower-filled, stone-wall-enclosed gardens beneath. It was Italian in its sunniness, its warmth, color and poetic sentiment. The guard came and we walked down a roadway, beneath an arched gateway and through a short tunnel, emerging finally into a narrow lane hollowed from the mountain side, with path continually ascending. Over us was the glorious blue; upon either side the walks; nodding at us from above countless wild flowers, stately acanthus and floral bells. We entered the "galleries," which are smoothly cut tunnels, perhaps ten feet wide with a height of twelve or more. At intervals, open portholes give light and also afford some exquisite miniature pictures of the world below, which seems so far away. These rock galleries were begun during the great siege over one hundred years ago. They turn and constantly ascend. We climbed up and up by a smooth roadway, stepping outside frequently to look at the wonderful, sunlit view. The guide said we ascended only about four hundred and sixty feet, and then the "thus far and no farther" was sounded. He assured us they were all alike and could we go farther we would see no more, save that "in the open upon the summit the view was very fine." From the last and highest portholes we looked down upon three cemeteries for the whole garrison, all grouped together, although separated by low stone walls and iron rails. In a small enclosure laid the uniform, coffin-shaped graves of the Jews, apparently all alike. Next the multitudinous crosses of the Romanists, and then the large, orderly, flower-bordered enclosure in which many an English heart was sleeping. From the last we looked from crest to base of the almost perpendicular face of the loftiest portion of the Rock, but it made one's head reel. Once a year, we were told, upon the Queen's birthday, the highest gun is fired, those of the galleries follow, and the batteries all along the shore prolong the roar. Let us hope no more serious, simultaneous discharge than this will ever be demanded from this, the greatest and strongest fortress in the world. Then we walked gayly down, and drove through the lights and shadows of the weird tunnelled way and out into the sun-bathed, flower-garlanded lane, to the old Moorish castle, now a prison, which has defied the changes of twelve centuries;—and all, *all*, with the one I love best!

THE GATE BY WHICH WE ENTERED.

(*Concluded.*)

The town of twenty thousand inhabitants,— the Alameda or public gardens, Esplanade, batteries, drives, and in fact everything which constitutes Gibraltar as a settlement, lie upon the slope at the base of the western face of the Rock, for the simple reason that the eastern side, rising abruptly from the level plain known as the neutral ground, is perpendicular, the south rugged and almost so, and the north too precipitous for any such lodgment. The drive to Europa Point, the extreme southern end of this huge monolith, ridden and torn for purposes of warfare and strife, yet peaceful in its billowy outlines, its gilding of yellow gorse, and its jungle of tropical and gorgeous floral growth, was like a prolonged fête or "battle of flowers," for it was a way whose salient characteristics changed so rapidly, whose detail was so rich and varied, whose natural and artificial attractions were so numberless and beautiful, that the memory of it is a jumble of colors, effects and exquisite picturings. At times along an ascending roadway, with tree branches forming an arch overhead, and through the shadow-flecked vista perchance a red-coated figure or two, or a heavily and picturesquely loaded donkey plodding its way, or some vehicle with white curtains or natty English drag or tasteful victoria. Again, upon one side may be high walls or villa terrace, and, coquettishly bending over and nodding at the passer-by, an enormous mass of scarlet or great balloon of pink ivy geraniums or lovely saffron, white or pink roses, while, upon the opposite side, you may look over the low wall and in a ravine-like depth see cool sago palms and yews and flowers and flowers beyond counting. It carries one through the lovely Alameda or Public Gardens—once a burning desert—called the "red sands," but converted, as far back as 1814, into a garden and improved from time to time, until now it blossoms like the rose. This large tract upon the hill-slope is laid out with drives in every direction and the whole enclosure made to seem more extensive than it really is by the covering of the entire surface with a thicket or jungle of beautiful shrubs, aloes and huge mounds of geraniums and roses. At the entrance is the Esplanade or Parade ; a large, level, open plaza, and along the sea-front of this stretches a long narrow tract, charmingly enclosed, through which walks are carried as between continuous flower-banks, with flowers, flowers of every variety and every tint, everywhere, save upon the paths, leaving scarce a square inch uncovered. The road passes through also the old Southport gate—a huge structure of stone with two arched passage-ways, with the arms of England over one, and some old Moorish and Spanish crests over the other. The approaching road is much elevated, so that at one side one looks down exquisite green depths with lovely palms and tropical trees, and upon the other, over a sunken graveyard, exquisitely beautiful, being full of quaint tombs, fairly buried in roses and geraniums, with the high wall continued from the gateway, a solid and unbroken mass of luxuriant ivy and great swaying branches of blossoming roses. The wild flowers, of which there is an immense variety, not to be outdone, crown every hummock, toss to and fro upon every wall and crowd upon the very drives much as the gamins push to the front and occupy every coign of vantage whenever there is a circus or military parade. Private houses were actually concealed by riotous growth of the branching ivy and an avalanche of brilliant blooms. Count-

THE GATE BY WHICH WE ENTERED.

less flowers too, from their positions, seem to have sprung up spontaneously and with the unchecked fecundity of weeds. Always high above us the topmost ridge with its crown of the Signal Tower, "El Hacho," or torch, because there in the olden days, the warning fires were lighted in times of peril; always about us queer ravines and batteries, odd structures with flowering plants pendant from their summits or sides, and blossoms innumerable of tropical and temperate climes; and when the eyes were fairly wearied and bewildered they could rest continually upon a cobalt stretch of waters, and beyond, upon the wind-tossed-like mountains of Africa lying against the blue sky, as peacefully and placidly as if guarding our own heavenly Lake George.

It is a fine, smooth road all the way and amazing in its variety. At the Point we walked beyond the line to which carriages are allowed, but the charm was in the view. The day was absolutely perfect. The great Rock presented an entirely different appearance. Across the waters, the ever-fascinating shadowy African range was neither amethystine nor opalescent as before, but simply a blaze of refined color, while the more distant heights were a heavenly, a soft, dreamy blue. They fairly waved and throbbed, and something within us responded harmoniously to the lovely rhythm. The solemn eloquence and suggestiveness of this peerless scene can never be quite forgotten. Doubtless the clear skies and atmosphere and the glorious sunshine accentuated its loveliness. Doubtless the finest view around Gibraltar is attained from "El Hacho," the Signal Tower, to which a zigzag road leads up the steep western face, but it was not accessible during our sojourn. To stand upon this rugged mountain eyrie, and with one sweeping glance to look from the snow-crested Sierra Nevada range, and the glorious nearer hills of Spain, down upon the blue Mediterranean and upon the Atlas Mountains of Africa, all throbbing with color and glowing with sunshine, must be a sensation for a lifetime!

We drove back, often by ways we had not seen, and, passing through the town, went to the opposite extremity of the Rock and upon the level, unattractive "Neutral Ground." From this the frowning mountain seems like a gigantic boulder rising from the level almost sheer and perpendicular to its greatest altitude. Its expression is decidedly combative, for, high upon the face of the gaunt gray rocks, are visible portholes, tier above tier, with here and there a battery. There it stands looking toward Spain as if its back was up and there was not the slightest intention of forgetting it! What a red rag is to a bull must be the bloody flag of England waving over it to every Spaniard—a constant aggravation, an imbittering and undying irritation. For it is in every sense a port of Spain, yet as a common "valet de place" said, "but for the English, Gibraltar would be a second Tangier in its degradation and barbarism."

Every day just before sunset a squad of four men passed the hotel down the principal street, one leading, then three abreast and one bringing up the rear. The central one of the three carried a large ring with the cumbrous keys of the city gates. They stood facing the gateway a few moments in military precision,—a gun somewhere in the fortifications was fired, and then the inner and outer gates were closed and locked for the night,—a foot-passage to one side being left open a while longer. And this mediæval-looking ceremony is observed every day in the year! Said a friend, when some months ago we were planning our itinerary, "Gibraltar is a good place to get away from. A day is more than you will care to spend there." But given such brilliant, exhilarating weather and such picturesque and floral conditions as characterized our visit, weeks could have been delightfully passed there. The place is so unique. There is but *one* Gibraltar! The exigencies of modern warfare will never demand another. It is even said, because of improvements, inventions and changes in military movements, the place is not as impregnable as reputed. Its history sounds like romance! Think of this great Rock being for eight hundred years the bone, for the possession of which Moor and Spaniard continually fought! When "the one-eyed Berber"—the first invading Moor—conquered and took possession of this mighty Rock, so unlike the adjacent coast of Spain in character, he bestowed upon it his own name "Gebel Tarik," mountain of Tarik. Evolution is a mysterious process at best. As scientists and theologians are lost in attempts to follow it in their respective lines, it is scarcely worth while for us to even wonder how this degenerated or developed into the modern cognomen "Gibraltar," the synonym of defiant power and impregnable strength. The Moors and Spaniards played battledore and shuttlecock with it, until, in 1704, the English took it, ostensibly for the claimant to the throne it supported, but, true to her instinct, she managed to keep it for herself. Yet as one reads the story

Gibraltar.

of the great four-year siege and defence, one feels she fairly earned it by her heroism, pluck and endurance. But it is an expensive possession; for it is said, one billion, two hundred and fifty million dollars have already been expended upon it, and it costs five million of dollars annually to support. It adds also not a little to its interest to read that, way back when the Phœnicians regarded this the end of the navigable world, somewhere here was established "Calpe," one of the pillars of Hercules, while upon the opposite African heights several hundred feet higher, was that of "Abyla," the Mount of God, in their vernacular, but called by the English "Apes Hill."

* * * * *

A lovely Sabbath afternoon we sat in the flower-crowded garden bordering the Esplanade. On the opposite side of the thicket some thirteen scarlet-coated soldiers and several ladies were singing a hymn preparatory to an open service. The voices were sweet and harmonious, the effect pleasing. In a place where every characteristic, every prominent feature was suggestive of kingly power and royal sway, it seemed peculiarly appropriate to sound out upon the air as they did, again and again,

"To Him all majesty ascribe
And crown *Him* Lord *of all.*"

AN OUTLYING POST.

"THE CITY PROTECTED BY THE LORD."

Although in no sense a portion of the country of the little King, Tangier, in Morocco, is so convenient of access, and withal so novel, oriental and interesting, that almost every one who "bides a wee" at Gibraltar makes an excursion to it as part and parcel of the regular Spanish campaign. As the way to it is by the sea—never a royal road —individual experience and narrative may be directly contradictory and yet be conscientiously correct. For some will lugubriously tell of wretched steamer, "scarcely better than a cattle boat," and of "a horde of Barbary Jews," of tempestuous waves, cloud-capped or concealed mountain range, and a final landing from small boats upon the backs or in the embrace of swarthy, greasy Moors, while others will talk gayly of "good ship so and so," of sunny seas, of mysterious opalescent African heights and of an exquisite picture of clusters of pearls with setting of green, of emerald and blue of sapphire which "the city protected by the Lord" seems, as approached. Both in going and returning we were fortunate in happening upon the largest steamers, having also smooth sunlit waters, a lovely panorama of the African mountains and the low lying Spanish shores, once in clearest atmosphere, again in soft delicious haze, and the blessed privilege of stepping from the cumbrous hulks which met us at the anchorage, a full half mile from the shore, directly upon the rude elevated footpath which juts out upon the sands like a miniature bridge,—having, too, the warm sunshine throughout the day and the white moonlight at night and the clearest and tenderest blue of sky unto the end! What wonder, then, that it is a sunny memory, oriental and romantic in its suggestion and coloring? The morning we left Gibraltar the atmosphere was deliciously hazy, quite unlike the day when first we beheld the mighty Rock with every outline and every detail as clear cut as a cameo. The low hill shore of the straits, and undulating stretch of loveliest, tenderest green, and the African mountains trembled, dreamy and opalescent as a continuous bank of mother of pearl. Even the Lion lost some of its grimness and looked sleepy and dull. Along the shining waters we passed as by a path of gold. Little appearance of occupancy had the green rolling hills, save, at long intervals, the humble habitation, and everywhere the confines of the fields marked by hedgerows of huge aloes.

Ancient interesting stone watch-towers are still standing at short distances—a reminiscence of a race and régime of a far away past. Yellow gorse alone broke the stretch of living green. Until some two hours later, when we came abreast Tarifa, we saw not a hamlet or village. In that soft dreamy atmosphere the little town, apparently walled towards the sea, with its irregular outlines, its flat-roofed houses and the Point beyond with its lighthouse, was simply enchanting, and all,—because the sun shone! The first Berber sheik who landed in Spain bestowed upon it his name—Tarif. Just here it is quite the thing to note, with all the unconscious "chic" of an original discovery, that here in "ye olden time" the Barbary pirates and officials kept watch of the passing vessels, compelling each to pay tribute, and from this name and fact comes our modern word "tariff." All writers do it,— hundreds of diaries note it, and a myriad of home letters scatter the fact far and wide. Here the steamer's course was changed and we crossed directly the bay of Tangier. Ere long a white spot, indistinct because of the haze, was discernible, and at four o'clock the ship cast anchor a half or three quarters of a mile from the shore and "Tandja, the city protected of the Lord," laid before us in an amphitheatre formed by the slopes of two hills, white, dazzling and picturesque against a blue sky. Only those who saw the "White City" of 1894 can imagine the peculiar effect of this grouping of glittering whiteness, relieved only by the distant green of foliage and the profound blue of the sky. Citadel and town make a confusion of white cubes standing loosely and at every angle with here and there a tower or a stately palm. Out came a swarm of boats with picturesque Moorish or Barbary oarsmen. Such a rabble! Such a chatter! The queer-robed figures from first to last afforded endless amusement and brought us quickly over the dancing waves to the frail elevated foot pier—and we were "in darkest Africa." A moment later we entered a portico or arcade, where we saw at once four handsomely attired Moors cross-legged, literally "sitting in the receipt of custom," solemn in their dignity and impressive in their stolidity. Unfortunately in our hands was an innocent box. It must be opened, and then one of the great swarthy fellows looked from his seat and, without gleam of intelligence or change of countenance, waved us peremptorily to pass on. Up a narrow filthy lane or street with pavement, compared with which a good honest cobble-stone pavement would be smooth, we tugged to Hotel Continental—well located and with views from windows and balconies over the bay and beach and the dreamy distant hills—quite like unto Naples.

After lunch we mounted sorry and melancholy looking mules, and attended by a figure so brown of skin and so voluminously draped in dark coarse burnous that he could well have posed for an "Ishmaelite in bronze," we began an experience so unique, strange and varied that the day will always be a red-letter day to us. Down narrow lanes, along the principal streets, through arched gateways, past mosques and whimsical little six-by-eight shops and up hill and down, through a motley crowd of all shades of brown faces, from black to copper, and all sorts of draperies from dingy white to duskiest brown, we passed, emerging finally in the great Market Place and open space upon the hillside. The first look was bewildering, for it was a scene, novel, weird and strange. Hundreds of robed and heavily draped figures, with here and there a red fez relieving the dim and dingy mass, were moving to and fro, gesticulating, shouting and calling their wares. Upon the ground lay the hideous camels, all around heavily laden tiny donkeys and uninteresting mules,—hundreds of the drapery enveloped figures showing only bronzed faces and legs, while cut grass, vegetables, fruits, bread and rude pottery were spread out in apparently inextricable confusion. For awhile we watched the antics of a snake-charmer, with hideous accompaniment of indescribable noise. The whole scene fairly dazed and bewildered. It was a first glimpse of oriental life, and with it came the thought that it was to just such a multitude the Master came with that mysterious love of His, and that it was the common people who heard Him gladly. It seemed as if He might have stood here and sounded out the glad words, "If any man thirst let him come unto Me and drink." We tarried a long while moved and impressed by the strange ghost-like scene, and then, along a narrow country road, with sides lined with enormous growth of cactus, aloes and bamboo, we gradually ascended the hills beyond the city. Frequently an iron screen or fence would reveal a villa, very Italian in tone, and give a glimpse of the flower-embowered gardens surrounding it. At one open gateway we entered and dismounted, and lo! we were in a second Eden,—"Huerta de Hardan" the suburban villa and grounds of the Belgian Consul. It was a large enclosure with wide, straight gravel paths in centre crossing at right angles. Roses in richest profusion like dwarf shrubs, and, climbing the tree branches, falling over in showers of bloom, yellow jasmine, ivy geraniums, heliotropes, marguerites and many curious tropical flowering shrubs were loaded with blossoms. Palms and tropical trees, and on every side a perfect jungle of lovely flowers, until it seemed as if we had been caught up and allowed for a little while a suggestion of the Eden man ignominiously lost. Through the thickets a white draped Moor occasionally added to the novel effect. Standing at the entrance of the villa, the eye swept beneath palms and fringe-like trees, over a snowdrift of marguerite shrubs and along a waste place brilliant with yellow mustard, to a bit of the deep blue sea, overlooked by a castellated tower. Mounting the mules we pulled up the hill. The light was beginning to slant. It would have been absolutely quiet but for the oft repeated "Go on, you blackguard," of those who attended our mules. To one side, we overlooked a beautiful rolling hill country as verdant as if covered with growing grain, and there, walking slowly across the fields were two solitary draped figures,—suggesting those common fishermen on their way to Emmaus. Upon the hilltop was an open plateau above the city literally carpeted with dwarf purple and crimson vetches. The view was superb, not only of the rear of the city, the mountains beyond the bay, but the Straits of Gibraltar, the bay of Trafalgar,—where every Englishman, as was expected, did his duty,—and way out over the dreamy, hazy blueness of the sea. All around this plateau, behind walls and buried in verdure, were villas of the wealthier classes. We paused at a well. A young girl with a huge water bottle stood by. Filling it, she poised it gracefully upon her head and passed on. What wonder, in the hush and stillness, we thought of One sitting by Samaria's well, preaching, in simple every-day imagery and word, the little sermon which to-day has the freshness of eternal spring! The sun had fallen low and, as we turned city-ward, cast long shadows of us upon the descending slope. Patient sheep were nibbling the succulent and vetch-covered carpeting;—in the distance, here and there the draped figures moved to and fro, and over all was a hush deep and solemn, and yet it was not "Holy Land" but only the suburbs of Tangier, the capitol of Haabit, the political diplomatic court of the empire of Morocco, with a population of fifteen thousand souls. In returning we passed through some very droll lanes and streets in which many a picture was framed, such as a Moorish archway with two or three mysterious figures in as many positions; a green Saracenic entrance with a child in rose-pink with white burnous sitting in the open doorway and picturesque forms all along the crooked way. We were told there were few Moors in Tangier, for they despise it. The majority are Barbary Jews. A few official Moors are here because obliged to be. The street life is peculiar. Tiny little shops open to the thoroughfare, piled with wares, are on every side, while within lolls or squats the one in charge. Many are at work embroidering, hammering metal, etc. The majority of the people are thin and gaunt with a bloodless look, yet they do not seem lacking in vitality, as is shown by their gait and speech. The large number of old faces would indicate that, hard as the life seems, it does not exhaust rapidly. One evening we visited the swell café of the Moors.

A glamour and romance invest these places in the imagination with a charm and glitter rarely realized, for they are often very shabby and matter-of-fact, although interesting. Ascending a side staircase with "rises" faced with rude blue and white tiles, we entered a long room with ceiling of wood and through the centre a row of arches, the columns supporting which were faced with crude colored tiles. A tall dado of gay matting encircled the room. Upon the walls were richly painted and decorated gun racks and brackets, coarse plaques and musical instruments and—shades of the Moors! four narrow oblong *chromos* and an *electric light!* Some twenty-five Moors (no Jews would be allowed to enter) were sitting in picturesque groups upon the floor smoking and playing cards. They were barefooted, for their shoes are left at the entrance where a rack or shelves are provided. To one side in the centre four or five musicians made the night hideous with instruments and vocal recitative. At one side of the entrance a little kitchen furnished place for endless coffee-making. But it was a little incongruous to serve it in English china breakfast cups! It seemed a life that is impenetrable, and yet, as we sat there wondering if there was no way out or up, the chromos and electric light seemed as evangels, for had not these features of modern life crowded in and been adopted by this ancient and well-nigh effete one? There is nothing like an entering wedge, even if as commonplace as this, for the Kingdom is surely coming! Another cloudless day we descended to the seashore and rode a mile or two along the yellow sands. With our backs to the city the scene might have been along the Maine coast or the Jersey shore. The waves lapped lazily, the air was hazy and the mountain outlines dreamy and delicate. But along the curve and across the golden sands were strange, mysterious figures moving along, and dull and heavy camels plodding their thankless way. A mile away we came to the ruins of an ancient Moorish castle. Difficult was it to analyze the weird mystery of the scene,—the strange feeling that a life strong and throbbing, as represented by these walls and battlements, has so completely disappeared from the face of the earth. But over it, the blue sea, the phantom hills, the soft lapping waves and the lovely color of water and of sand seem to breathe a sweet and solemn requiem. Later we climbed the higher ridge which dominates in the rear, that in the shelter of which Tangier stands. There was little that was novel save some groups of thatched African huts. After some two or three miles we reached a high point commanding an extensive view of nearer and distant mountain ranges and the shimmering sea. Finally we stopped at the estate of the "Governor of the Port," which, unlike others we visited, seemed devoted almost entirely to fruit of all kinds with here and there a few flowers. We were met by a handsomely dressed and courteous Moor, who at once took the lady of the party to call upon the Governor's wife. In a little while he returned and invited us to the terrace, a crude affair, well shaded, but with a view of sea and mountains fascinating and enchanting. Coming up a path we saw a little Nubian slave, black as midnight, perhaps ten years of age, dressed in a rose-pink jacket over which was a thin muslin slip, with enormous hoops in ears, and bracelets, anklets and rings, carrying a salver with cups and teapot and a plate of bread, in slices as thick as your thumb, with a layer of butter an eighth of an inch thick! The tea was already sweetened and flavored with sprigs of mint and lemon verbena! It was romantic but not perfect, for the cups were English china and the teapot Sheffield plate! It was blissful, however, to sit there and sip the tea, and, looking beyond the Nubian slave, see the soft blue of distant mountain and quiet sea.

Lastly, we visited the prison in the town. It was inexpressibly sad. We entered a large dismal room, with, on one side, a barred door or window, with an aperture of perhaps twelve inches in diameter, through which we looked into a court with a number of wretched creatures. As they have only what their friends bring to them we thought to distribute a handful of Arabic coins. It was horrible, for all we could see was a wild, wriggling, scuffling mass of outstretched hands and occasionally a bit of a face, with a noise that was simply demoniacal. It was the only discordant note in our sunny visit to Tangier.

Those who make, as many do, this excursion in November or the winter or early spring months, will look askance at this story of a visit in sunlit May days, with everything propitious, as a fanciful and a "to be taken with an allowance" tale. Yet it is none the less truthful. One who has not been in the Orient, but who has often pictured it in imagination, will, in the life of the streets, the grotesque little work-shops, the market place, the picturesquely draped and turbaned figures and the conceited camels, recognize many a characteristic and receive many a suggestion of the detail and environment of the never tiring Gospel story. In fact, there were times when, to us, Tangier faded quite out of sight and in thought and feeling we were far away among the " Holy Judean hills."

OUR FIRST SPANISH TOWN.

Opposite Gibraltar, across the glistening waters of the bay, beyond an ugly fleet of black dismantled but anchored hulks, which serve as coaling stations for the various steamers, but very suggestive of some recent naval engagement, lies, white and low upon the shore, the town of Algeciras, important to us as the terminus of the railway, the modern Pegasus which was to bound with us up and over the hills, and, by repeated connections, carry us across central Spain to San Sebastian upon the extreme northern frontier. Our glorious weather came suddenly to an end. In the early morning the sky was not promising, but a clear patch of blue here and there gave us hope of at least a gray day. On the wharf it sprinkled, on the bay it rained, and the rest of the morning it poured! So our exit, our departure was entirely devoid of those multitudinous elements of the dramatic and spectacular which made our entrée so charming and delightful. But the great rugged "mountain of Tarik," gray and sombre, drizzling and wet, with occasional pearly clouds drifting and shattering against it, was grand and majestic, defiant and leonine to the last. From the jaws of the stately monster we walked immediately upon landing into the capacious maw of the Spanish Custom-house. A droll appearing train awaited us. The road is an innovation of late years. The bed did not duplicate that of the Pennsylvania railroad as it crosses the Alleghanies, but we were fairly comfortable, and we *were in Spain*, where for many a year we had builded castles like the temple of old with sound of "neither hammer nor axe nor any tool of iron." For a while our way lay through a valley with gentle hills on every side. The wild flowers were abundant, and often the fields were carpeted with great patches of crimson, mustard yellow, blue and purple, and frequently were brilliant with myriads of scarlet poppies. Ere long we were conscious we were upon an up grade, through a lovely rolling hill country. Stone pines in great groups, cork trees, knotted, gnarled and quaint, beautiful glistening oaks, orchard-covered slopes, great aloes and prickly pear, gave, upon the verdant surface beneath, a great variety of form and color; while here and there flashed the low, one-storied, whitewashed Spanish houses or an old watch tower. Even upon this insignificant road the stations were made attractive and pretty by an enclosed garden at either end with fences buried in a wealth of roses and other blossoms. In two hours we were high up in the very heart of the mountains. The scene was not, of course, as overwhelming as in the Swiss ranges, but it was very beautiful, and at times really grand. We were lifted up as upon a ledge, high upon the hillside, and looked down into depths where a little stream was breaking into foam, and up and up to the summit of the opposing heights. It was raining, and the heights above were often indistinct or lost in clouds. While we would have preferred seeing them basking in joyous sunshine, we consoled ourselves with the feeling that probably they were more impressive and fine in the misty air. In some places most peculiar narrow clefts were visible which geologists say are the effects of erosion. Some look as if a narrow slice had been cut clean out with a knife in some giant hand. As we neared the summit we passed through a succession of tunnels and began the descent to a richly fertile and highly cultivated country. Oh! how beautiful it was, with its grain fields, dark olive orchards and upon far-away hillsides the gleam of many a white villa, and beyond, the glorious hills! In descending to and approaching Ronda, the railway describes a great lordly, sweeping curve like unto a capital " C." " Would you stop at Ronda ? " we asked, some months ago, of a popular author familiar with the route. "No," he replied, "you will see all there is from the train." It seemed presumptuous in face of this to stop, but sundry photographs in the shops of Gibraltar had made our desire to see the place, the magnificent bridge and the strange cliff and ravine, too strong to be denied. To this day we fairly hold our breath with thought of that we so narrowly escaped losing, for it was not only "Our first Spanish town," unspoiled by modern innovations, but the lay of its land and its deep romantic ravine were strikingly peculiar; while the outlook and view from the edge of the cliffs upon which it stands, both near and distant, were superb and grand. A few minutes ride in a " 'bus " brought us to a unique little hotel in the centre of the town, with a porte-cochère leading to a patio or small open court, in the middle of which was a quaint well-curb and crane of iron around which were large shrubs in great jardinières. Two arcades surrounded it, upon which the rooms opened. All this became commonplace afterwards, but never lost its picturesqueness and interest. At lunch we were introduced to the Spanish custom of cooking everything with oil, to which we never became quite reconciled. Otherwise the "menu" was palatable and good. We found the long vistas of the streets extremely pretty, being very white and every one with the most ornamental, tiny frame-work of iron called "rejas" around the windows with a roof and bracketed supports, many with glass sash close to the trellis-work. The effect was very pleasing, as it is like an abundance of small oriel and bay windows hanging to the sides of the houses. As we looked down them, men with full Spanish cloaks, women in picturesque costumes, or dashing figures with "sombreros," gave a characteristic and national look which was charming. We quickly sought the celebrated bridge over the "Tajo," or chasm, or ravine, which is *the* sight of Ronda. The town is built upon an elevated rock or plain upon the edge of a sudden and abrupt precipice, in some places one thousand feet in height. By volcanic action this has been cleft in twain making a narrow gorge or ravine some two hundred feet in width. Over this, connecting the modern with the ancient Moorish town, is the magnificent stone bridge with one lofty, stately central arch, with, upon either side, resting upon higher foundations, a smaller one. Through this ravine the little Guadalvin (deep stream) breaks over a rocky bed, and in its tumultuous course girdles, at the base of the precipitous heights, the little town. Open spaces in the stone parapet, guarded, by wrought iron grilles, give a fine view of the ravine depths some six hundred feet below. Mills, mules and workmen below look like toys. That Ronda has fallen into line is demonstrated by the electric plant of the town resting upon ancient Moorish foundations, way down this ravine. The view upon one side is contracted because of the abrupt curving of the ravine, but the sides of the "pudding stone" formation are, by action of waters, columnar in outline and effect. Upon the other side the scene is most varied and picturesque, little white buildings being perched among the rocks, while waterfalls and cascades break over the bed in whitened foam, and stretching way beyond, is the green Vega or valley. Over the bridge and through the old Moorish town we passed on our way to the depths of this wonderful chasm. It was by a donkey path, muddy, pasty and slippery, following the face of the precipice, ever with lovely view of the valley, and turning suddenly at last, revealing the mighty chasm in all its breathless magnificence and beauty. At point after point we paused for a few moments, quite certain that outlook was the best, only to find the last and the lowest "led all the rest." The scene is a wonderful combination of the natural and artificial, the two being so blended and harmonized one hardly notices where one ends or the other begins. Upon either side rises, sheer and abrupt, to a height of between six or seven hundred feet, the walls of this strange ravine in all shades of yellow or brown, with here and there a touch of green or dash of brilliant wild flowers. Connecting the two is the bridge some two hundred and seventy-six feet above the waters, a noble piece of masonry of the same tawny hue. The bed of the ravine drops suddenly a hundred feet or more from the foundation ridge. Standing in the lowest depths the picture is grand and impressive. The great precipices, tawny and yellow, streaked with brown, seamed, scarred and discolored by the storms of centuries, rise in oppressive grandeur:—the peerless central arch or bridge frames in a bit of blue sky and a white cottage upon the cactus-crowned cliff beyond; upon the edge of the cliffs at the right appear a row of picturesque, irregular white "casas" or cottages with overhanging belvedere gardens, and below the arch tumbles a single slender waterfall. The water breaks upon and disappears amid a mass of disordered boulders, then in whitened foam breaks and falls in another fall into a grotto-surrounded basin. The tawny heights glow here and there with brilliant wild flowers,—the dampened boulders display rich russets and browns, and, in front of the grottoes, like graceful draperies, hang trailing vines. At the last the troubled, whitened, foaming waters pass through the arched foundations of numerous Moorish mills. Beyond is the level valley, a placid sea of tenderest green. The old Moorish town, with its queer, crooked streets and its white houses, pretty " patios " full of roses and flowers and with belvederes overlooking the valley and commanding the distant mountain ranges, being novel, simply enchanted us. We visited the ancient " Casa Mandogon," now uninhabitable, belonging to the duke of the same name, with a vestibule opening into a lovely court with moulded red brick arches supporting the storey above, having also a curious well, with environing shrubs and vines. An inner court has arches and columns with exquisite incised and colored Moorish tiles in the spandrels and an ingeniously carved balcony of wood. The roof timbers and supports of the corridors were beautifully and daintily carved, while at intervals the thick layers of whitewash were scraped off, showing the exquisite incised work which really covers all the walls. One room had a ceiling of tiles set between elaborately carved beams, and was girdled with a dado of pretty antique tiles. We went up stairs and down,—the rooms being empty,—admiring ceiling and the novel general effect, and stepped out upon two belvedere gardens overhanging the sheer precipice. The view was superb, for, like a flattened bowl, from six hundred to a thousand feet directly beneath us laid the valley, every foot of which was vivid with green of wheat or brown of fallow land, with here and there a white farmhouse and everywhere the winding roads with patient mules and overladen donkeys, looking like playthings, toiling along. In a wheat field was a threshing-floor—a perfect circle in the living green. Way beyond it all are the mountains that are round about pretty Ronda. The panorama of hills is said to be one of the finest in Europe, but low lying clouds prevented any other view than the nearer ranges. Occasionally they would lift momentarily, giving us a delightful glimpse of that, the full glory of which was hidden from our eyes. An ancient cathedral full of Moorish and Roman architectural features and odd and unique details, with gilding executed three hundred years ago, but as bright as if done yesterday; the oldest bull ring in Spain, one of the things every one wants to see once,—when vacant; and a charming alameda or Public Garden with lovely flowering shrubs upon the very edge of the cliff, and commanding a superb view, made us feel that with the bridge and romantic ravine one could not "see all there is from the train" passing a good quarter of a mile away. As we passed away, the lifting clouds afforded a fine farewell view of the mountains. For twenty miles we looked at an old Roman aqueduct borne upon tall arches,—like the vertebræ of some extinct leviathan. Then for seven hours we passed through a country richly diversified in character and surface. Miles of beautiful olive orchards, vineyards, thousands of ilex or oak with glossy foliage and graceful form, and in some places great, bare, gray mountains, which, as the sickly sunlight touched at times, seemed as if covered with snow. We were in Andalusia, the garden of Spain, and were simply amazed at the height of cultivation, the look of prosperity and the beautiful aspect of every orchard-covered hillside. The mountains were always with us, at least along the horizon, and we continually looked through solemn olive orchards and long rows of stately stone pines upon their shadowy, billowy and rugged forms. There was little sign of life; occasionally a herd of goats, a few sheep, but no cattle, and frequently a scarlet-sash-girdled countryman with a sombrero. Great tall, stiff poplars, ruined castles and towers, white-starred and red poppy fields, with men ploughing with grotesque Roman ploughs of wood, women along the way with railway signals, great banks yellow with buttercups, and slope and slope of billowy hills dotted and shadowed with olive trees, and distant views of rugged mountain heights, filled up the measure of the happy day, until, at closing, the rain and mist made all blurred and indistinct. . . .

In a patter of rain and darkness which might be felt, we drove in the evening through the streets of Granada, and climbing the Alhambra hill, passed unconsciously through the celebrated avenue of elms,—the royal road we had expected to see in full glory of silver sheen, suffused with romantic and poetic sentiment, for the moon was at the full.

A MOORISH LEGACY.

To lie down to sleep at night, entirely ignorant by sight, of environment, with sound of drenching rainfall and outer darkness obscuring or obliterating all detail of surrounding; to awaken in the morning to unclouded sky of serenest blue, to a world flooded with glowing sunshine (and that world, the enclosure of Alhambra fortress walls), to look down upon garden court of glistening glossy foliage and blossoming flowers, —down a hillside with stately avenue of overarching, interlacing elms planted by the immortal Wellington,—with plash of fountain waters and note of nightingale and song of joyous bird, and air redolent with perfume of roses and honeysuckle, is an experience, a sensation never to be quite forgotten. It was like awakening after the trouble and sorrow of an earthly to a new existence,—a heavenly sphere! Such was our induction to the charmed enclosure of the red and glowing encircling walls and the fairy-like lights and shadows of the wonderful Moorish legacy of the Alhambra. Notwithstanding the graphic descriptions and exquisite word-pictures of various gifted writers which have become "classics," few find, upon arrival, their ideal a correct one. The story of the Alhambra should be read with a ground plan before one, just as the itinerary of a country should be followed upon a map. There is no need for giving here statistics or historical data, for they would only be borrowed and are better stated elsewhere. But it is not, perhaps, amiss to emphasize that some three miles of massive walls, intersected by huge square towers, enclose the summit of a high hill overlooking the ancient city of Granada. Within this area are gardens, terraces, two large hotels, a village, a cathedral, half ruined towers, the unfinished palace of Charles V.—a long waste place, and occupying really a very small proportion of the space—the remains of the old Moorish palace, the structure to which the mind reverts at sound of the word "Alhambra," while in fact the whole fortress is called by that name. Even then it must be remembered that the fairy-like beauty and exuberant ornament, so associated with and recalled by the name, are confined to the interiors. The outer walls are utterly devoid of comeliness or picturesque outlines, the towers and buildings being mostly square or angular, with flat roofs, and windowless. This bare and almost unbroken exterior is said to be " to guard against the three great enemies of the Moor,— the heat, the evil eye and the projectiles of enemies." But from the opposite heights their red and tawny walls, in some places thirty feet in height, following all the irregular surface of the hillside, with the towers and block-like structures, look singularly and strikingly beautiful, especially when seen against the white flashing slopes of the far-away snowy Sierra Nevada range. Alas! the ravages of war, the upheaval of the earth, the rapacity and neglect of conquering forces and the slow remorseless decay of years have obliterated much of this, considered by high authorities, the most beautiful structure in the world. But the romance, the poetry, the picturesque history, just as the perfume of the roses hanging about a shattered vase, cling to it still, and make it one of the most enchanting and delightful visions upon the earth. It was the morning of the sixteenth of May, after a night of rain, that we awoke to sound of nightingales upon every side and the glad consciousness that we were, as by magic, within the charmed precincts of the storied Alhambra. At an early hour we sauntered out, paused at once as we looked down, fairly entranced, upon a stretch of park-like greenness with wealth of stately trees, with, near by, a group of bric-à-brac and flower venders, and farther on by huge fountain bowl, several women with dash of scarlet and yellow in costume, with brass utensils and crude pottery, a picture of rare beauty. We walked along by wide handsome roadways through thick woods or shadowy glades, with here and there the white foam or soft plash of fountains with the sunlight tingling through the great elms and the lights and shadows dancing with bewitching, fascinating effect upon the sward,—and all the while, the glad exultant cry in our hearts, "The Alhambra! the Alhambra!" Up the hillside we climbed besieged and followed by an importunate bevy of dark-eyed, yellow-skinned gypsy women and grotesque little girls with flowers and pretty, graceful, dancing ways, till we stepped into level gardens with profusion of box borders and myrtle and other trees and faced the great unfinished palace of Charles V. Scarcely any other structure in the world has so many maledictions poured upon it as this really fine, but uncompleted, palace! And why? Because to make room for it, much of the old Moorish palace was destroyed, and because it is so out of tone and keeping with its surroundings that it is a blot upon a fairy scene, a discordant note in a lovely harmony. An earthquake so unsettled it it was never roofed in. With its great rough block foundation storey, its beautiful pilasters and renaissance windows, anywhere else, with its medallions and bas-reliefs, it would be admirable. We passed with scarcely a glance at that time, for beyond another garden gorgeous with blossoming acacia trees and blooming roses (the famous place of Cisterns), rose before us the Torre de la Vega, or watch tower, from which one of the finest views in the broad world is obtained, and it was a day of days for it, the air being wondrously clear and transparent. This old tower, like all of the Alhambra pile, has no external beauty, being devoid of any enrichment or ornamentation. The name suggests a tall campanile, but this is only a great, massive, square dry-goods-box sort of an affair, perhaps sixty or more feet square, with smooth, yellow brown walls pierced here and there with unadorned window openings. An interior staircase conducts to a flat paved roof guarded by a wall or plain battlement. From one side rises a simple belfry with a bell which gives to the farmers on the broad fertile plain the signal for turning the waters of the river upon their lands through the irrigating canals. Here also an inscription records the first raising of the Christian flag in 1492, after seven hundred years of Moorish occupation and possession. But, oh! the view from it! It is of breathless and incomparable beauty and may well be called "the most beautiful in the world." After sitting there a whole morning we felt earth might possess a fairer, but surely not a more impressive and lovely scene. All suffused with the brilliant and glorious sunshine directly beneath us was the dense foliage of surrounding gardens, several diminutive, flower-laden terraces, and here and there a tower or glimpse of wall. Farther on lay, at the foot of the hill, the proud city of Granada,—a myriad of Spanish grooved tile roofs, a flat mass of white, blue and russet, broken only by delicious, cooling greenness of shrubs and trees, with the grand Cathedral rising tawny and golden above them all. Beyond stretched like a map the marvellous Vega—or level valley called "the last sigh of the Moor,"—verdant beyond picturing, cultivated, well watered and fertile to the last degree, broken only by the darker hue of orchards or trees, the shadows of passing white clouds or the white gleam of villa or hamlet walls.

Along the horizon the rolling hills or bounding mountains, and in the opposite direction against a blue sky far above the nearer hills, the cold, white, flashing range of the snow-covered Sierra Nevadas. Light clouds, like smoke, floated lazily over their white faces, recalling the "touch the mountains and they shall smoke" of the Psalmist. The Sierras present a tame outline as compared with Alpine peaks, but their glorious whiteness above this scene of eternal spring is exhilarating, awe-inspiring and impressive. No wonder the vanquished Moors wept as they looked back for the last time over this vast and lovely plain, as they passed over the white Sierras to perpetual exile!

They told us that in a few weeks the fresh green would be tarnished and burned, but that day it was simply enchanting with its marvellous freshness and verdancy and the cloud-like phantom mountains showing in dim, gray, shadowy outlines beyond. No wonder Charles V., leaning from one of the windows, is said to have exclaimed as he beheld the glorious panorama spread at his feet, "Ill-fated the man who lost all this." As our stay lengthened and we became more or less familiar with the entire enclosure, the views from the numerous windows, the outlook from the various towers, possessed a charm and fascination for us not surpassed by the exquisitely ornamented courts and "salons" we had travelled so far to behold. One day we passed out of the gates, down the hill, crossed the Darro in the valley bed, and ascended an opposing height to the plaza of the church of St. Nicolai. Hitherto we had looked only *from* the Alhambra, but now we looked towards it, as upon a panorama long drawn out, a scene unique and characteristic and unrivalled in all Europe, as

> "It rises o'er Granada's hill
> And from its height looks proudly down,
> The guard and glory of the town."

Grand and impressive rose the steep hillside, verdant, densely wooded and with open, orchard-like spaces, crested with the processional, ruddy walls, the tawny, orange, angular towers and a tumbled, confused mass of roofs and buildings, with a cathedral spire, and, lifted far above against the warm heavenly blue, the dazzling white Sierra range. While not as beautiful as Heidelberg, it is a lordly and regal pile. The long stretch of irregular walls, broken by frequent towers, have a strange motion, as of a mighty army marching forth to war. As a mass of color it is unique, for the deepest and tenderest greens, the glowing red, the richest orange and soft yellow, blend in beautiful and lovely harmony against the background of blue and pearly white. The points of interest within the encircling walls are widely scattered. At one extremity stands the Gate of Justice, so familiar from earliest childhood by book illustrations as to seem like the face of an old friend; a huge, square, clumsy structure pierced with a double-arch passage, with the well-known sculptured hand upon one, and, upon that above, the key, of which the Moors proudly declared, until the hand grasped the key, the Alhambra could not be taken. It was the place where Moorish Kings— as in the Orient to-day—held open-air court of justice for rich and poor. Almost at the other end are the two towers of the Captiva and the Infantas, both beautifully restored, which, in delicacy of decoration, beauty of design, almost surpass anything in the old Moorish halls. They are so light and graceful and airy, that, standing within them, one seems lost in dream or fairyland. One can scarcely go astray in the enchanted enclosure. Of course one must "do" and see it all, but it is a blissful moment when, having made the lovely round, one can wander to and fro according to his own sweet will. For whether sauntering in the wooded park-like approach, basking upon the sunlit terraces, dawdling in the gardens, hanging over the walls, or dreamily wandering through the deserted halls, all is a delight. In the place or Garden of the Cisterns, always lying in wait, seeking whose "pesetas" he might devour, was the Gypsy King, with his proud distinction of having been a model for Fortuny and Regnault. His lithe, wiry figure, flashing eyes, alert movement and picturesque costume of black velvet with crimson sash, made him in such surroundings interesting, but his insinuating manner and glib impertinence were intolerable. Yet as an element of the picturesque, he toned in prettily with the dreamy, sleepy, romantic character of the place.

A MOORISH LEGACY.

(Continued.)

SOME months before our departure from home, we were looking one evening at a collection of photographs of the most celebrated architectural wonders of Spain and expressing our individual idea and imagination of them, when a lady, familiar with the country, remarked, "If you expect to see the Court of Honor of the Columbian Exhibition repeated in effect or extent, you will be woefully disappointed, for the Alhambra is not imposing or immense, it is simply delicious!" Being thus forewarned and forearmed we were spared the disappointment we would have felt in the lovely architectural creation of the ancient Moorish Palace of the Alhambra, for we imagined the apartments much larger, when in fact the whole suite of peerless, fairy-like rooms is exceedingly small. Otherwise they were all our fancy painted them, and in many respects far more poetical, mystical and beautiful than our wildest dream. A lovely afternoon we passed into that fairy-like domain for the *first* time, out of the hard prosaic world of to-day, into a realm where beauty, imagination and romance hold high, mysterious and fascinating carnival. The change in a single moment from the dull, ugly outer walls and court to the celebrated "Court of Myrtles" or of "the Blessing" (a rectangle some one hundred and forty by seventy-four feet), full of sunshine, which the rich creamy walls seem to absorb, with a long pool or cistern, bordered with a low hedge of myrtles, with an occasional Japanese medlar or other shrubs, flashing with gold fish and reflecting the lovely arches and surrounding intricate wall ornamentation, was magical and bewildering and enchanting to the last degree. At first it was quite enough to simply *be* there! to lose oneself in the delicious air of perfect quiet and absolute repose: to feel the delicate fairy-like thought enshrined and crystallized in the ornamentation on every side, filling the mind and heart like strains of sweetest music, and the warm sunshine making glad and joyous the mysterious whole. The side walls are comparatively plain; but at one end rises in three tiers the loveliest arches, windows and loggia, with exquisite ceilings, all covered with the exuberant, floriated and profuse geometrical ornamentation which is the ruling characteristic of the Moorish style, while at the other, above and beyond an ornate portico or colonnade of elaborately decorated arches and slender columns, rises the huge, massive, battlemented "Tower of Comares"—or Ambassadors. What this all must have been when overspread with rich, brilliant colors, intermingled deftly with riotous addition of gleaming gold, is beyond imagination or dreaming. But we wondered, gorgeous, opulent and sensuous as it must have been, if it could have surpassed the refined, delicate effect of the present dreamy softness and mellowness of color, as if saturated with the golden sunshine. We found, with every visit, that the entire suite of courts and apartments grew and unfolded like a gorgeous tropical flower, revealing fresh beauty and loveliness at every turn. With the exception of the Court of Blessing, the Court of the Lions, and the Hall of Ambassadors, the apartments seem surprisingly small. But oriental life has never demanded the wilderness of incongruous things which make our occidental drawing-rooms labyrinths of furniture and museums of bric-à-brac. Only after repeated visits could we look at these emblazoned walls and embellished apartments, without hopeless bewilderment of vision and feeling. Then it became a beautiful harmony, sweeping us captive, far away into the land of imagery and sunny day-dreams. Yet some tourists "see it all in a day," and one lady at table d'hôte could not be reconciled because the intricate, marvellous, incised decorations of the walls were not cut in marble, instead of the adamantine plaster or stucco. From the Court of Blessing one passes into the Hall of Ambassadors beneath the Tower of Comares, the only apartment which approaches the designation of grand, imposing or sublime. It is but thirty-seven feet square, but the domed ceiling of rich dark wood, a labyrinth of intricately interwoven geometrical carvings, cunningly inlaid with stars, discs, crescents and rays of pearl, like a firmament studded with constellations, is some seventy-five feet above the pavement. With its lofty walls daintily and elaborately decorated, showing, inwrought with the geometrical lines in the most unexpected places, the Arabic characters signifying "There is no conqueror but God,"—heavy stalactite cornice, rows of deep embrasured windows filled in with frost-like arches and exquisite screens, each framing in a lovely and finished picture of the outside world, a dado or "azulejos" of superb tiles, it is indeed a regal, lordly apartment, fit to enshrine a proud, royal throne. We had looked at the summit of this tower with inexpressible longing, but the ascent to it is not generally allowed. Finally, after innumerable words and considerable diplomacy, our friend, who for thirty-five years has lived in Spain, secured permission to visit the roof. A narrow, rickety staircase, often wholly dark, led to it. As we anticipated, the view upon every side is breathless in extent, beauty and interest. One side overlooks directly the Court of Myrtles or Blessing, with its great green-bordered pool, like a huge mirror, reflecting the graceful arches and wondrous ornamentation. The scene is so serene and holy that it is difficult to realize the bloody horrors history tells us were enacted here. The best idea of the general ground plan of the whole palatial pile is obtained from this elevation. It is a motley confusion of rough tiled roofs, with a glimpse of the "Court of Lions," and that of "the Oranges," that one looks down upon with no revelation of the beauty it enshrines, suggesting rather a house added to and added to, whenever the erratic owner had anything to expend. High above the irregular roof appeared a church and tower, the palace walls, great trees, and way beyond against the warm blue of sky, the eternal, perpetual whiteness of the Sierra range. To one side was the Court of Oranges, a shoal of greenness in the dazzling white, with pretty loggia, and the windows of the rooms occupied long years ago by Washington Irving, acacias, cypress and a tall basin fountain. Another court showed the low, droll, pierced domes of the baths, while the Court of Cypresses with paved enclosure was a veritable apotheosis of the much despised cobble-stone. From the opposite side one looks to a depth of six or seven hundred feet below, and off upon the city with a multitude of curious lookouts, or loggia upon the roofs, and a myriad of brilliant enclosed miniature gardens, and upon a hillside burrowed with the huts and habitations of the gypsies,—a most fascinating scene. Upon another, the eye rests upon the red walls and massive towers and a great terraced garden with geometrical lines of quaint, stiff box, with glowing masses of gorgeous roses and clouds of white syringas—and then beyond, over the great sweeping valley—brilliant with sunshine and flecked with many a cloud shadow. Almost adjoining this tower, quite hidden by an insignificant building, is a miniature mosque of extreme delicacy and fabulous beauty, with indescribably beautiful carved and gilded roof, fine tall dados and enriched arches. It is a glory of azure and scarlet and burnished gold, and is a favorite subject and background with artists. Near it is a small patio or court, finely restored, with arches, marble columns, façade and cornice fairly covered with intricate, lace-like designs, and inscriptions cunningly inwrought with the florid and graceful conceits.

When this regal fortress passed out of the control of the Moors forever, the incoming Christian powers covered the lovely walls which were so rich and sumptuous with wonderful incised, colored and gilded ornamentation, with several layers of whitewash, or plaster, in order to obliterate the texts from the Koran so frequently incorporated (which, however, were good enough for Moslem or Christian, either one). It seems like sacrilege,—a bit of pious vandalism! So the taking of the fragmentary frieze of the Parthenon, long years ago, by Lord Elgin to England, may also seem. But those precious fragments and specimens of Grecian art would long since have been burned for lime, destroyed, lost forever, but for Lord Elgin's appreciation and action.

So in this rude covering of the Alhambra walls has lain their preservation and safety, and we owe it to the vandalism of opposing religions that they are in existence to-day! Through all the conflict and strife and changes of years, and the even more fearful, because insidious, destruction of neglect, the faithful plaster, chrysalis-like, has imprisoned and preserved this rich legacy of a dead past, until, within comparatively few years, infinite patience, enthusiastic skill and loving research, have as it were carved them afresh, to be a joy forever.

> "Brightest gem on Moslem brow,
> Brightest wreath by Christian won,
> Brightest shade of greatness gone."

A MOORISH LEGACY.

(*Concluded.*)

FROM the poetic stillness and enchanting weirdness of the stately Court of Blessings or Myrtles, one passes beneath low arches, crosses a narrow corridor, and *the heart stands still*, for at glance, in all its glorious beauty, flooded with golden sunshine, lies before him the famous Court of the Lions, a veritable Holy of holies in this fair and sumptuous tabernacle of architectural loveliness. The familiar photographs and engravings, while faithfully portraying the beautiful groupings, exquisite details and fairy-like general effect, convey an erroneous impression,—that of a much more extensive and spacious enclosure. The regal court always *seems* small! It is easy to say it is a rectangular court—one hundred and twenty-six by seventy-three feet in extent, surrounded upon all sides by a low, cool arcade, with slender, delicate shafts of marble, so softened and yellowed in tint as to seem of onyx or alabaster, exquisite, graceful capitals or arches, spandrels and wall face covered with infinitesimal, intricate, oft-repeated designs of marvellous grace and variety, with at either end a little square porch, much like a pall of richest guipure lace, projecting into the open sunlit space, in the centre of which stands the famous fountain, an immense bowl sculptured from a single block, supported by twelve conventionalized and grotesque Lions. That is what you *see* in the bewilderment and confusion of surprise and delight, but it does not picture it, for it is indescribable. It is the "dolce far niente" of architecture! The airiness, grace and phantom-like effect cannot be portrayed with words. It does not awe, overwhelm, repel or oppress as many a mighty architectural thought wrought in stone is apt to do. It simply enthralls and enchants with its riotous luxurious and sensuous grace and elegance. It is a song, a poem, that tingles long in the memory, when perhaps the solemn prose of some mighty structure has lost its hold. It is a place for the artist, the poet, the dreamer, for a hard-headed, matter-of-fact person would pass through it, and, likely, brush all this exuberance, riotousness and elegance of ornamentation out of existence, with a sweeping "overdone," or "too much of it." Perhaps there is danger of its cloying some prosaic palates, with

The Alhambra, Court of Lions.

its linked sweetness, much crowded and yet long drawn out. It is one of the places in the world, where one of appreciative mind wishes to be alone, to sit in the cool shadows of the quiet arcades, or even in the glare and stillness of the open court, and let imagination and sentiment hold the reins, to see that which is suggested and not simply that which is material. Entranced, spell-bound and enchanted, one may sit by the hour in that matchless, dreamy, peerless court, without grasping the *ignis fatuus* of its charm and beauty and yet be saturated, filled to the overflowing with its wondrous glory and delicacy of form and detail,—its fancy, thought and feeling, fixed forever in imperishable design. It ceases to be a building,—it melts into a dream, dissolves into a fairy illusion! Sitting there, with the sunlight coming and going, resting upon the consummate traceries or passing through the pierced openings, it seems like a flock of beautiful white birds of exquisite plumage that has alighted in its glad flight for a moment, and which at any time may spread their golden wings and disappear from sight. Again, the wind action and play of frost-work seem to encompass one around and about, occasioning almost a terror or fear lest, in the warm glowing sunlight, it may dissolve ere its beauty is fixed upon the mind. Again, the walls seem covered with richest and costliest embroideries; soft, creamy altar lace seems pendant between the delicate arches. It is a bride, all glorious, adorned for her husband! Surely this heavenly vision of intricate, sumptuous ornament of matchless and suggestive grace,—this weird procession of slender columns, glowing as if within their hearts they held absorbed long centuries of sunshine, cannot be reduced to words! Arrested, petrified beauty and loveliness alone express, as of solemn Alpine heights, the sentiment and significance of that rich, mellow, voluptuous scene. With impressive beauty that cannot be delineated, stands in the centre of the unbroken enclosure, the beautiful bowl, sustained by the grotesque lions. O'Shea says they "must be looked upon, not in a sculptural way, but heraldically, as of emblems of strength, power and courage." It is well to remember this, for otherwise these whimsical representations would require the explanatory legend oft placed beneath a child's drawing, "This is a Lion." It is all as still and peaceful as if human life had not been brutally disregarded also here, and its very stones stained with human blood. The ugly facts of history will obtrude upon this vision, with its dream of fair women and brave men. Little domes and towers rise above the low sky line, and the blue sky and floating clouds beyond resolve it into a dream beside which the tales of Arabian Nights fade into insignificance. There is no sign of life, no suggestion of motion save the dear little martlets,—the only birds held sacred in Spain, because they drew the thorns from the head of our suffering Lord,—which fly to and fro, twitter and disappear in the intricate open fretwork of numerous spandrels. To see, as passing clouds may permit it, the sunlight come and go upon the delicious, creamy groundwork, to watch the reflected light as it strikes the inner arches and porticos, and to note the blue of sky through the floriated open work and lace-like spaces, is bewildering and fascinating beyond expression.

To one side a portico opens into the well-known "Hall of the Abencerrages," to which is attached a horrible story of blood and carnage, fortunately, largely legendary and unreliable. It is a stately and impressive room with alcoves upon either side, a gorgeous, pendant, stalactite ornamented dome and a fountain in the centre said to be stained with blood. The side walls, above a superb dado of raised and colored Moorish tiles, are a solid mass of intricate floriated and geometrical designs. Through window arches in the dome filters a soft dreamy light, giving a most unreal and frost-like look to the whole superb apartment. Directly opposite, and opening in the same way upon the Court, is the "Hall of the Two Sisters," so named from two large slabs set in floor or pavement. The interior is the culmination of all that is mystical, poetical, suggestive, harmonious and bewildering in the whole extensive pile. Some one has truthfully said "a petrified veil of the most delicate lace covers every wall, formed partly by flowers and geometrical patterns, but in the main intention of its fretwork as strictly religious as the sculpture of a Gothic cathedral, and filled with sentences and maxims from the Koran, which it is intended to bring constantly before the eyes and hearts of the beholders." Alas! as one reads of the life around which this structure rose and which it enfolded, it is impossible to ignore the old maxim, "Familiarity breeds contempt." Perhaps, as in the case of a brilliant architect, who inscribed among the sumptuous decorations of a ceiling in his house a text of Scripture so utterly at variance with his record as to call forth the cynical surmise that "he put *all* the religion he had upon the wall." This exquisite apartment, designed for the Sultanas and their slaves, defies description. Not a foot of wall or domed ceiling space but is a study of delicate, intricate and lovely design. Alcoves, recesses, windows, arches, galleries and dome are loaded with the richest decoration conceivable. A wonderful ceiling, composed of some five thousand pieces, hangs and droops in graceful stalactites as in the Cave of Luray. A sumptuous dado surrounds it, windows appear above filled with exquisite screens of wood, and all through the bewildering ornamentation is inwrought an oriental poem. While the room is square, the arrangement of the vaults and domes is such that the lofty ceiling is octagonal. It stands like a bride enveloped in richest and costliest lace,—a wonder unto many. Through an opening is seen a tiny boudoir, a perfect gem, into which, looking through three arches which seem hung with rich lace, the eye rests upon a superb wall surface like heavy embroidery of gold, pierced with two graceful openings through which gleam the trees and flowers of the Lindaraja. Across one end of the Court of the Lions is the Hall of Justice, a long apartment of seventy-five feet, so divided by arches, alcoves, etc., as to make a suite of seven richly adorned and decorated rooms,—a most superb vista. By many, because of the minuteness and delicacy of the wall ornamentation, these are considered the finest of all. Yet in a general sense, they but repeat the others, save that in the elaborate decorative designs, by command of Queen Isabella, is inserted the yoke and arrows of the Catholic Kings and the oft recurring legend "Tanto—monta," which is said to be old Castilian, meaning that one is as good as the other,—Ferdinand as good as Isabella. Curious and interesting are the Royal baths, a number of small rooms much adorned with exquisite tiles and the wondrous stucco work. One, the place of repose after the bath, has been so beautifully restored, colored and gilded as to be the loveliest of all. It is very charming, having two alcoves with elevated couches, marble columns supporting an ornate gallery for musicians, a central fountain, and over all a lovely ceiling much adorned. A little outside gallery led us to a modern decorated boudoir of the Sultana—surrounded by a loggia,—overhanging the walls and commanding a most picturesque view of the Darro, and the city and hills beyond.

* * * * *

In the official bureau flanking the entrance, we were shown an old register with the autograph,

"Washington Irving, 1829." It was a peculiar gratification to be allowed, later, to visit the suite of rooms occupied by him in those years so long ago, by royal consent, and in which much of his literary work relating to the Alhambra and Spain was executed. They are entirely different in character and decoration from those of the stately courts and sumptuous "salons." All overlooked a small secluded court, now dark with sombre cypress and glistening orange trees. Two of the apartments (one of which was his working room) were large and spacious, with lofty, deep panelled ceilings of dark wood, while three or four had low ceilings covered with scarlet and gold mouldings, which formed hexagon spaces in which were painted fruit and flowers. Were we surfeited with the wonderful interlaced scintillations of Saracenic genius upon the palatial walls, or was it the triumph of mind over matter, the eternal survival of the fittest, that these rooms, so sombre and insignificant, compared with the regal halls through which, as bewildered as if in fairyland, we had wandered, possessed an interest and magnetism to us none others held? No wonder a fair young girl ran back for her miniature copy of Irving's Alhambra, that she might feel that, for a few moments, at least, it had been in the room where its text was penned! Ah well! the tale of war and carnage,—the romance of intrigue and deceit, the glamour of beauty and courage, and the poetry of love and gallantry with which the very name "Alhambra" is saturated, must pass away, but the beneficent work of our genial and gentle Irving will live and grace the homes of men long after this lovely fabric will have crumbled into dust.

SOME GRANADAIN FRAGMENTS.

AROUND every great exhibition there clusters a variety of attractions (we call them "side shows"), some of which we would not like to quite forget. So, although the Alhambra dominates everything at Granada, around it are many objects none the less interesting and entertaining. Perched upon the steep hillside beyond the Alhambra and overlooking it, the city of Granada, and way off over the plain, and in fact "all creation," is the "Generalife," probably originally a watch tower, then a summer palace or villa of the Sultans, but now, by marriage settlements, the unoccupied possession of an Italian Ducal family. As the rambling buildings, romantic loggia and quaint towers (only a small part of the original), surrounded by a succession of embowered terraces, shady nooks, flower-crowded, sunlit courts, with fabulous profusion of roses and blossoming shrubs, cypress and flowering trees and fountains, it far surpasses the Alhambra in everything save the lavishly decorated interior walls. In the freshness of early morning, in the glorious sunshine, we passed along the Alhambra hills, crossed a little glen, and ascending, soon entered a tall, iron gateway and walked along a road bordered upon either side with hedges full of lovely roses, then into a curving path of great beauty, closely lined with tall, sombre cypresses, trimmed closely and pyramidal in shape. It was as hushed, mysterious and sombre as a place for the dead. The gray of the pathway, the sombre, dense green of the tall cypress trees and the blue sky far away, with the wealth of golden sunshine, made a beautiful scene, recalling Whittier's

"Alas for him who never sees
The sun shine through the cypress trees."

We came into a small insignificant court, made glorious by a palonia tree, bowed down with great wisteria-colored blossoms, passed through a low wooden door, and lo! a perfect paradise; a long, rectangular, open court laid out in box-lined flower-beds, with water-jets everywhere and plants, shrubs and rosebushes covered with brilliant blooms. At one side rose a wall fifteen or eighteen feet high, which, in turn, supported another terrace above. Against this, orange trees with golden fruit, immense rose-bushes, heavy with blossoms, and a variety of climbing plants were smoothly trained. One mass of blood-red roses covered a space of thirty by fifteen feet. The great branches, with hundreds of the gorgeous red roses, swayed in the breeze or laid against the wall in solid mass of color, startling, brilliant and gloriously beautiful. Upon a little terrace above, a wall was covered with the tiny, saffron cluster "Banksia" roses. Against a column where we entered was a mass of "Marechal Niels" so graceful and abundant as to almost seem artificial. Opposite the entrance, at the other end of the court, was a two-storey loggia with the airy, decorated Moorish arches and columns, entwined and garlanded with the loveliest white and yellow roses imaginable, and everywhere, through the warm colors of the blossoms and the cool green of foliage, visible in the wall ornamentation, the oft-repeated "God alone is Conqueror." Opposite the cloud of blood-red roses was an open loggia or corridor faced with low Moorish horseshoe arches, having upon the outer side a succession of window openings. Leaning out of them one overlooks terraced gardens with noble evergreens, quaintly trimmed cypresses and a wilderness of flowers, down and down, and across the verdant and wooded valley to the orange-red walls of the Alhambra, with its pile of roofs and massive towers, and beyond, over the Vega, the eye rests at last upon the mountains that fade out of sight in the hazy air. From this we entered the villa and passed through several rooms, with curious inlaid ceilings of wood, unfurnished save a number of portraits of no artistic merit. Every window commanded some fascinating outlook over little flowery terraces beneath, and the distant country. A few steps up led us into a wide corridor with arches, against which great rose vines tossed a cascade of golden and dazzling white. Each column was a mass of foliage and blossoms, and overhead trailed and swayed the great yellow and white roses. From it we looked down upon a great square open court, overshadowed by curious trees, with long cisterns or pools, fountains and vases, and, as always, a lavish wealth of flowers. At the opposite end a gateway, surmounted by lions and a crest, led up a stone staircase lined with potted plants, into a terraced garden with box borders and view after view, enchanting and bewildering. Then through embowered "allées" into an elevated loggia with, below, a court shadowed by cypress, the soft drip of waters and plash of fountains, flashing of gold fish in the sunlit pools, and always, always the cloud of golden roses. From

Garden of the Generalife, Granada.

this loggia the everlasting hills loomed up upon one side, eternal springtime upon the other, while solemn cypresses rose against the bluest of skies. Up and up stone staircases with queer little water ducts upon the balustrade, with the rapid flowing waters of the Darro, we went to a terrace with many potted plants and a higher tower with loggia. As we looked from it we wondered if anywhere in the broad world there was any that excelled it. Immediately below,— terraced gardens with wealth of color, magnificent acacias and roses, drolly trimmed cypress, stiff, quaint box borders in geometrical lines, a great tree bowed down with purple blossoms, queer busts of majolica upon tall pedestals, and across the glen the glowing fortress walls, and beyond the wondrous valley, shadowy mountains, and always overlooking the scene, the cold, gleaming, snow-crested Sierras. To one side the olive orchard hillside, and above it all an old ruin upon the heights, called the "seat of the Moor." From there it seemed as if the kingdoms of the world were spread out. The view of the Alhambra is so satisfactory, for one can follow the contour of its walls, see its various towers and all the world beside! Way across the green valley plain, basking in the sunshine, is historic Santa Fé, from whence Columbus, after years of effort, turned away discouraged, only to be recalled by Isabella. At our feet to the right rose the hill, burrowed as by rabbits, in which the gypsies live, Afar off a gravelled plaza, now dark with trees, is memorable as the place where the last Moorish ruler, Boabdil, gave up the keys and passed over the Sierras never to return again. And all this in one sweeping glance.

So many writers speak of Spain as barren, cheerless, desolate and treeless, that it was an agreeable surprise to find, all the way from Gibraltar to San Sabastian, a stretch of greenness,—a "battle of flowers." Gibraltar was a glory of color, Andalusia delicious with olive and orange groves and verdant hillsides, Granada, Seville, Cordova and Aranjuez, garlanded as for a fête, and even the waste places along the railway a blaze of scarlet poppies.

In the shadow of the encircling Alhambra fortifications are the gardens of Señor Calderon, enclosed by three miles of wall. Forty years ago it was a barren, rocky hillside, but an expenditure of a million of dollars has made the desert place glad, so that it blossoms like a rose. The extensive enclosure is a labyrinth of rose-hedged paths, long grape-covered arbors, lovely resting places beneath great trees and numerous terraces covered and overwhelmed with roses, orange flowers and other blooming plants. Through charming, winding paths one comes at last to a great terrace laid out in Italian style with angular borders, fountains and statuary. Up and down we passed to terraces with enormous palms and evergreens, with orange trees white with blossoms, and air heavy with perfume, with wide-spreading lindens like bowers, and all the while the peerless outlook over the Vega and distant mountains. Peasant houses, great thickets of laurels, and high walls hidden by huge, solid masses of golden Maréchal Niel and pure white roses, gave charming variety. A high, red, rough wall suggests some old castle ruin, but a staircase to the top reveals, irregular in shape with island in centre, the costly reservoir supplied by a private aqueduct from the Sierras, which keeps this earthly paradise ever fresh and green. As with almost all Spanish estates, the villa is a modest affair just meant to sleep in, for the shady terraces give life and refreshment.

We drove out of town to the Archbishop's summer palace, surrounded also by lovely gardens. It is called Zubia, and is memorable as the place where Isabella narrowly escaped capture by hiding in a thicket of bay trees. A marble statue of her now graces the spot. Saffron Banksia roses covered a space of sixty feet upon the villa front, while yellow Niels and white roses fairly hid one wing.

The Alameda, a long narrow garden with at one end a bronze statue of Columbus presenting his plan to Isabella, is the fashionable rendezvous of the ladies of Granada, who pass to and fro in handsome carriages drawn by sleek mules—the aristocratic steeds of Spain. Quite out of the city is the Cartuja, a suppressed Carthusian monastery now held by the Government. There is little to see. Around a cloister are a series of hideous pictures of cruelties perpetrated upon the monks. The church is a wild chaos of rococo ornaments, with a showy high altar, and, in a rear chapel, a costly Ciborium or receptacle for the Eucharist, of cinnamon-colored marble. But worth more than all is a lovely bust in marble of St. Bruno, with the sweetest, saddest face imaginable. In the sacristy are some doors and ten great chests of drawers, a beautiful and curious combination of tortoise-shell, ivory and ebony, all wrought by former friars.

With feelings of peculiar interest we wended our way to the great Græco-Roman Cathedral, the first we had seen in Spain. But we were disappointed. A peculiarity of Spanish Cathedrals is, that the choir is walled in like a huge box in the centre of the nave, which prevents the grand and impressive sweep and vista which is the charm of English minsters and continental interiors. The lofty ceiling, the tall, classic columns and the fine gilded dome over High Altar were impressive. The pictures and details were interesting, but at no one point did we have the solemn, awe-inspiring and spiritualizing sweep one looks for in such large and stately structures. The royal chapel adjoining the cathedral, a church of itself, was the magnet which had drawn us thither. In the centre, between a tall superb wrought-iron "grille" and a high altar, with lofty retablo with exquisite bas-reliefs and sculptured effigies of kings, stand side by side the huge double mausoleums of Ferdinand and Isabella and their daughter Joanna (known as Crazy Jane), and her husband "handsome Philip of Burgundy." They are of white marble exquisitely and elaborately sculptured and surmounted by recumbent effigies of the four royal personages, but so high that the faces, which are said to be fine, cannot be seen.

Close to the iron railing which surrounds them, is the entrance to a vault below, in which repose their remains. With a feeling of awe, we descended the narrow staircase and stood in a low, round, arched apartment, in the centre of which laid two coffins of lead, bound with iron bands, one marked I. J. with a crown, the other F. and a crown, which contain, without question, as they have " never been disturbed by Goth or ghoul," the mortal remains of Ferdinand and Isabella. The coffins, wider at head than at foot, and with pitched or pointed roofs, look rude and battered. Upon one side, against the wall, is that of Philip of Burgundy, the identical one which his demented wife carried everywhere with her for forty-seven years. Upon the opposite side is that of Joanna, and at her feet that of her only child. No more pathetic story is there in Spanish history, than this of an unloved woman's insane loyalty and devotion. Isabella died far from Granada, but was buried here by her own request. So reposes the noble sovereign, with whom our own land is so intimately associated, who, as Lord Bacon says, " in all her relations of queen or woman, was an honor to her sex and the corner-stone of the greatness of Spain."

THE OVEN OF SPAIN.

STILL more commonplace and utterly devoid of romance or sentiment than our creeping into the Alhambra enclosure under cover of darkness and patter of rain, utterly oblivious of environment, was our rattling down the hill and through the streets of the ancient city in a close vehicle in the gray hours of very early morning, enveloped in dense mist and heavy downpour.

We had no farewell glimpse of ruddy wall or massive tower to make us want to come again. We had only a golden memory; and the Alhambra might as well have been a hundred miles away, for even its magic name seemed a myth. It was so cold and dismal, we were glad when, after seeing every piece of luggage securely wired or bound (because of recent extensive, unauthorized examination and reduction along the way *not in presence of owner*), we moved slowly away at half-past six towards pastures new. For four hours, when we reached Bobadilla, we passed over the same route by which we came to Granada. Now,

Bobadilla is a junction, a first-class crossroads in din and confusion, with a large restaurant, with everything cooked in oil. The least said the better. The journey in spite of clouds and rain was a beautiful one, for the mountains rose on every side and the views of country were fine. Between Bobadilla and Seville, a ride of some five hours, the scenery was very tame. Sometimes for miles we would scarcely see a tree of any kind, but only prairie land or gentle billowy hills in patches of all shades, from yellow to orange and russet, made by the fast ripening corn or grain. But everywhere was visible the highest cultivation, which seemed wonderful, in view of the very primitive character of the farming implements used. At times great herds of cattle or goats, horses or donkeys were seen upon the lonely stretch, in care of an overseer, often the only signs of life visible. A little after four o'clock, almost ten hours since we turned away from Granada, across the plain of living green, a long way off, we caught the gleam of numberless clustered roofs, above which possibly rose many a dome or tower, but we saw only the massive, stately, unmistakable "Giralda." Ere long we were in the midst of pretty villas, lovely gardens and thickets of dark trees or lustrous-leafed shrubs, and between stone walls and a yellow, muddy river, the Guadalquivir of our school days (rather more musical than the same name "Big River" in our vernacular), and then a dingy railway station, and we were in Seville, "the oven of Spain." The "oven" was only warm, but within the week of our sojourn it became at times uncomfortably heated. The usual customs examination at the station over, we crowded into a clumsy "'bus," and, with little ceremony, were hurried to the Hôtel de Madrid, said to be the best in Spain. Built around a large open court or "patio" filled with tall palms and graceful tropical trees, a jungle of creeping plants and brilliant flowers, with a central fountain and a honeysuckle-covered trellis like a great Greek cross overhead, above which, in the heat of the day, an awning was drawn entirely across, and with double galleries overlooking, with pleasant rooms and unexceptionable "cuisine," it was altogether the most charming and delightful hostelry that sheltered us in sunny Spain. Although the day was far spent, waiting until another, with the famous "Giralda" only a short walk away, was not to be thought of, especially as it was "with sunset glow" we had been charged to see it.

The walk along the principal street of little shops, at either end of which stone posts make it impossible for carriages or vehicles to enter, and across two public squares and narrow streets with many a little bazaar entirely open in front, as in oriental towns, brilliant with golden and gaudy fabrics, was full of picturesque interest and fascination, not exactly conducive to rapid progress. The sudden termination of a street brought us face to face with the ugly, forbidding wall of a nondescript structure, pierced with an arched gateway, once richly sculptured, but now badly dilapidated, through which we passed at once into the oft quoted "Court of Oranges." How pretty and poetic it sounds! how dainty and ornate it looks in the numerous sketches and pictures! while in fact it is only a great irregular space, with many medium-sized orange trees and a fountain faced by open cloisters and portions of the ancient cathedral, with no expression save that of utter neglect and indifference, although the glimpses of rich windows, heavy piers and sculptured ornaments are extremely picturesque. Compared with any close, surrounding an English Minster, with its smooth lawn and venerable trees, its solemn, peaceful expression which seems to influence and prepare

THE OVEN OF SPAIN.

the mind to worship the Lord in His Holy Temple and in the beauty of holiness, this great court, which might be made as beautiful, looks little better than a play-ground or market-place. Against the cloister-wall is a small "bird nest" pulpit that looks very innocent with its whiteness intensified by the burning sun. Yet, from it has thundered forth much to incite the fearful "autos da fé" not far distant, by which thirty-four thousand souls were swept from earth as by a baptism of fire. Children were playing beneath the glossy orange trees, beggars were lolling around the fountain, cathedral guides were watching for their prey, and through the white cloisters lounged droll, shabbily costumed figures, a picture of Spain of to-day. Details, however, did not impress us upon that first memorable visit, for our gaze centred upon the Giralda, which rose so boldly some three hundred and fifty feet into the air, all aflame with the ruddy light and golden glows of the sunset hour. One rarely forms unconsciously a correct ideal of any structure from pictures and representations. This ponderous and majestic tower, at first glance, seemed so much greater and more massive and less lofty than we had pictured. It appeared ponderous and heavy and never seemed quite tall enough for its size. Perhaps we were too near, for much of this passed away with recurring visits and varied points of vision, till it stood in our minds with its gigantic stability, its Moorish conceits, its delicate details and its general impressive dignity as indeed the finest *tower* in the world. Not, however, as the most *beautiful*, when memory recalls, in its jewel-like beauty and soft gleaming colors, rising high into the blue Italian sky, that wondrous dream, Giotto's Campanile, beside the old Florentine Duomo, above the ancient Tuscan city. Seen above the orange trees, stately, imposing and lordly, it fairly takes one's breath away with the audaciousness and fearlessness of its design and construction. It seems the base, to a height of one hundred and fifty feet, is the original Moorish Muezzin tower, built in 1196, attached to the mosque, which stood upon the site of the present Cathedral. Alterations and additions in various centuries have carried it to a height of three hundred and fifty feet. These additions rise in some three or four richly ornamented and varied storeys with a lantern-tower, the whole crowned finally by a statue of Faith which revolves with every wind. Perhaps that is in perfect keeping with the word "Gerar" to revolve, from whence comes the name Giralda, but it does seem incongruous for Faith to be turning with every wind and wave of doctrine! The Muezzin tower is of a pinkish tint, ornamented with lace-like Moorish designs of sunken work, while dark tiles in long soft lines add to the mellow glory of color, and the modern additions are rich with dainty windows, classic balconies, curious ornaments of iron and stone. Upon the corners of the first platform is a queer conceit, an enormous bell of stone, surmounted by open globe-work and great vase of lilies in iron.

The ascent is most interesting, being to top of the Muezzin tower, by thirty-four zigzag inclined planes, so gradual, that one could ride upon horseback all the way. Above, marble and stone and iron staircases lead to the summit. One pauses often, for there is much of interest, and lifted so high in air, the eye catches many a lovely outlook, through the open-work or from the pretty balconies. While among the deafening bells, some special peal was rung, and it was most exciting and thrilling to watch the men hanging on ropes and swinging through the great arched openings, way outside of the tower as if performing upon a trapeze. Way up in the tower, in wretched little rooms, we found living a blind keeper, who stood with us, and turning his sightless eyes, pointed out the interesting features of the view with the greatest enthusiasm. Fortunately one of the party understood Spanish, else we would have lost this pathetic illustration. It is needless to add, we left him radiantly happy and invoking the blessing of the Virgin and all the saints upon our heretical heads. The view of the white city far below, with here and there a touch of blue, or roof of pink, and over the surrounding verdant plains and along the river's course is, in the morning sunlight, very peaceful and beautiful. Every New Yorker may not be able, at his own sweet will, to bridge the distance beween our great metropolis and sunny, pretty, far-away Seville and look with delighted eyes upon this wonderful architectural fantasy, but whosoever will may pause for a few moments on the southwest corner of Twenty-third Street and Fifth Avenue of a late winter day, when the west is all ablaze with crimson and gold, and, looking over the bare tree-tops of Madison Square, see rising, rich with reflection of glows and sunset hues, against a background of pale blue or delicate mother-of-pearl, the tower, of which this Moorish, Spanish structure is the prototype. Understand, it is not so large or great,—in one sense it is not as fine,—

but as an effect, to one mind at least, although it may be heretical to say it, it is more airy, graceful and beautiful, and in its way quite as enjoyable, as that which is the glory of the fair city beyond the sea. Yet I have stood there again and again, impressed and hushed by its beauty, in the exquisite atmospheric conditions of the hour, and, although an intelligent crowd was continually passing, have never seen an eye turned toward it in appreciative glance nor a footstep checked to note its picturesque and beautiful effect.

THE OVEN OF SPAIN.

(Concluded.)

THE exterior of the mighty Cathedral is a disappointment. Owing to a great mixture of style and the absence of the pitched roof inseparably connected with the name cathedral, it is very confusing. Until we ascended the Giralda, we could not grasp the ground plan. It is certainly very picturesque, but no other or marked impression is made upon the mind. Here and there are features and details of great beauty, but there seems no one point whence the building, as a whole, can be seen. The eastern apsidal end, with its roof balustrades and piers, makes a pretty and attractive picture. With the chapter-house, chapel and other attendant buildings, the cathedral is mounted upon a platform of three or four steps, with great pillars from ancient Roman temples standing at short intervals. It occupies the site of two successive mosques. Many an exquisite sketch can be made, for it is a regular crazy quilt of pretty details of half a dozen styles.

But over the entrance portal might very appropriately be written, Who enters here leaves disappointment behind, for the interior satisfies and overwhelms with the grandeur of its immensity, the harmoniousness of its design, the solemnity of its expression and the sublimity of its architectural effects. It is indeed a fulfilment of the declaration of a Chapter way back in 1401, that it would build a church "so large that coming ages may proclaim us mad to have undertaken it." Alas! only a few years ago an earthquake made sad havoc with it, utterly demolishing the central tower, or lantern, above the intersection of transept and nave, which in its fall carried or weakened much of the structure adjoining, so that now, this, probably the most grand and impressive Gothic interior in the world, is so blocked up with immense scaffoldings and huge props, as scarcely to be seen in its majesty and beauty. But that which one sees is indescribably grand and awe-inspiring! The plain columns, clustered around huge piers, rise up and up, in unbroken and faultless beauty, while the continued arches soar away into space with illimitable grace and charm. Seven naves, side by side, spacious transepts, thirty-seven chapels, rich with beautiful sculpturings, golden altars, jewels and silver vessels, with dim religious light streaming through some ninety-three windows of some of the richest stained glass known, with paintings by many of the best Spanish masters, a gorgeous choir and at the eastern end a sumptuous Royal chapel, represent its most attractive features. Only a glimpse, through an open gate in the high board fence around the scaffolding, is had of the profusely ornamented and decorated choir, carved stalls and magnificent, lofty, wrought-iron screen or gates. Even the pavement of black and white marbles represents an outlay of one hundred and fifty thousand dollars! And the dust lies thick upon carvings, ornaments and the glorious stained windows, perhaps to large degree because of the repairs. The east and apsidal end forms the Royal Chapel, a magnificent church, built to receive the remains of royalty. A superb iron screen blocks the entrance; the whole interior is overloaded with applied ornaments, and upon either side in niches high above the floor are seen the royal coffins, now covered with palls of cloth of gold with embroidered crests,—surmounted by crown and sceptre. One is said to contain the dust of the beautiful " Maria de Padilla," of whom the tourist hears more or less in Seville. Before the high altar, in a magnificent casket of silver,

Seville, Cathedral and Giralda

richly wrought in statuettes and floriated ornaments, are the remains of St. Ferdinand, which, dressed in royal paraphernalia, are shown but three times a year. Back of it was an ivory Virgin and child, presented by St. Louis of France and carried by St. Ferdinand in all his campaigns. The sacristy is a veritable treasure-house, for in presses are some two hundred priestly vestments, exquisitely embroidered in gold and colors, in convents in the fourteenth and fifteenth centuries; and in cases are statuettes of gold and silver, jewelled crosses and holy vessels flashing with costly gems, and the celebrated "Custodia" or receptacle for the Host, a tall temple of solid and deftly wrought silver. At one end hangs Pedro Campana's "Deposition from the Cross," before which Murillo used to sit for hours and before which he desired to be buried. It is related that once—when told it was time to close—he said: "Oh! wait until these holy men get Him down." It is most effectively hung, richly framed against a marble wall, with laurel wreaths and palms. It is sombre and hard, but so solemn the mind is filled with awe. The loving, caressing carefulness with which two old men in flowing robes of red and blue lower the dead helpless body, and the tenderness with which a man below supports the precious burden upon his shoulder and breast, are most pathetic.

The Chapter-house is another superb apartment, oval in shape, and with a lofty dome, all bewilderingly decorated in "plasteresque," or applied ornament, with also many delicately carved statuettes. Some lovely heads and an Immaculate Conception by Murillo also adorn it. The latter differs from all others in that the eyes are turned downwards. Looking at it and several others in Seville, one feels he must have tried and tried to paint his ideal ere he produced the matchless one that graces the Louvre. At the west end of the grand nave lies, in the pavement, a sculptured slab, which has an interest for the passing American, for it covers the burial-place of Fernando, the second son of Christopher Columbus, who bequeathed his library to the Cathedral and was given a funeral almost equal to a King's. In the Baptistery, wretchedly lighted, hangs Murillo's wonderful "St. Anthony of Padua." It is immense in size and richly framed. A French friar at our side truthfully remarked, "Nowhere else but in Spain would a picture like that be allowed to hang in such a wretched light." It was from this canvas, on the night of November 4th, 1874, that the entire grand and sublime figure of the kneeling saint was cut, and carried off. Great was the consternation and grief among the people. The government at once notified its ministers and consuls all over the world of the cruel loss. The picture was finally offered in New York to William Schaus, the art-dealer, who, promptly recognizing it, purchased it for two hundred and fifty dollars and presented it to Seville. It is so beautifully inserted that, only as the light strikes it aslant, can the line of joining be detected. The saint, in brown Moorish robes, is kneeling in his cell. Above, in a glory of cherubs and angels, appears the Infant Christ. A doorway reveals a cloister and gives the only light save the reflected glory of the vision above. The reflection of light upon the monkish robes is so strange, the kneeling figure in its forward bend so full of eagerness and earnestness, the outstretched hands so full of humility, of "in my hands no price I bring," and the foot so beautiful, that like many of Murillo's canvasses it forms a picture by itself, a fact recognized by the contemptible thief. But oh! the soft radiant glory of the heavenly vision! The luminous golden atmosphere, the cloud of witnesses, floating and circling around like the multitude of swallows about the Giralda, some well-nigh lost in clouds, others in gleesome, childish embrace, and moving incessantly up and down the golden way! In the centre stands the Infant Christ with outstretched hands, plump limbs, and gentle, loving face. It is only that of a pure, lovely, fair-haired child, exquisite in coloring, yet it seems imbued with loving sense of the joy it is bestowing. Somehow in the stillness of that darkened, dingy, shadowed chapel in far-away Spain, we seemed to hear, as we gazed long and well at it, the hymn we so often sing at home,

" Fairer is He than all the fair,
That leads the heavenly train."

The story is simply and effectively told. The figure of the Saint is eloquence itself, and the intense yearning in eyes, lips and even chin, as he catches a glimpse of the Saviour's face, appeals tenderly to the thoughtful observer, for who has not at some time felt it as he has meditated upon the Adorable Redeemer?

In another chapel hangs Murillo's "Guardian Angel," in which a graceful figure, in dull yellow robes, and with outstretched white wings, is leading a little child by one hand and pointing to the opening sky with the other. The lovely little face of the child is turned confidently upward, the expression serious but very sweet. It is a dear little figure, fresh, innocent and beautiful, with lovely eyes and single gossamer white garment revealing the little plump figure, and exposing one shoulder. The charm of the picture is the little child, and the lesson of the trustful accepting face seems expressed in the "Except ye become as little children ye shall not enter into the Kingdom of Heaven."

In the dim light of almost every chapel hangs some picture which would interest an art student or connoisseur, and in every nook and corner there is something curious or of intrinsic merit. To see in one sweeping view this stupendous interior, when cleared of scaffolding and ugly supporting beams, would alone be worth the weary journey across the sea.

CÆSAR AND PILATE.

OFTEN as we wandered spellbound through the halls, or loitered half-dazed in the courts of the Alhambra and looked at the mellow, cream-colored walls, we wondered what the effect must have been, when all the exquisite incised traceries were picked out with gold or laid in with gorgeous colors. The question was as near answered as it can well be, when we visited the ancient State apartments of the "Alcazar," the remains of the old Moorish Royal Palace at Seville. Probably the beautiful restorations do not equal the original combinations, but the effect is unique and gorgeous in the extreme. Way back in 1181 a palace was built, which was added to at intervals, in different styles, until it covered, with its courts and buildings, an immense tract of land. Some of these additions have been destroyed, and some fifty years ago the Moorish or ancient portion—the walls of which, like the Alhambra, were covered with thick whitewash—was restored by the Duke of Montpensier at an expense of fifty thousand dollars. It was for a time the residence of the Duke who married the only sister of Queen Isabella, and is now frequently occupied by the ex-Queen. The private rooms upon the second floor are rarely shown. But the great patio or court, the lovely corridors, spacious halls and beautiful rooms upon the ground floor which constitute the ancient Moorish portion, the most interesting part, is freely opened. The original ornamentation of walls, all richly gilded and colored, the ancient mosaics and the superb tilings make them a dream of the Arabian Nights, a scene of sensuous coloring and enchanting beauty. Gold, red and blue predominate. Through a superb gateway we entered a large open court, with clustered marble columns and boldly decorated spandrels and arches. The ceilings of the arcades and the doors also were of intricate geometrical designs, richly inlaid and gilded, while the dados were of exquisite mosaic-like tiles, in many places iridescent in tint and hue. The rooms seemed the more impressive, because the superb stucco and colored decorations were confined to a wide frieze, or the spandrels, the open spaces being left for tapestries. One long room, which, with alcoves, was the length of the court, had a superb and heavy panelled ceiling with great bosses and heads, all of cedar from far-away Lebanon. In this lordly, sombre hall St. Ferdinand—he who conquered Seville—breathed his last. We passed through several rooms, with arches and exquisite-colored ceilings, restored by ex-Queen Isabella ere she was driven from the throne. From a window in a corner room, in which several of the Montpensiers first saw the light, we looked out upon a lovely decorated court and a charming vista of six rooms, a shower of red and blue and gold, into the glorious Hall of Ambassadors. This, although not as spacious or imposing as that of the Alhambra, being gilded, ornamented and colored to the last degree, is simply magnificent. Back of it is a Royal banqueting hall with fine vaulted ceiling of dark wood. The vista or view from another corner room, through Moorish arches of soft coloring, across the Hall of Ambassadors and out into the sunlit arches in court, with columns and windows beyond, is superb. The gorgeousness and magnificence culminate in the Hall of Ambassadors, a square apartment with lofty cupola or dome with curious geometrically lined ceiling. Upon three sides, single arched openings reveal the gorgeous and unique interiors of adjoining rooms, while the other shows the spacious and magnificent court. The side walls are an unbroken stretch of exquisite repeated designs in richest gold and most brilliant colors. High upon the walls are small balconies with rich brass griffin heads for supports—out of keeping perhaps with the rest, but a very effective innovation. Dainty little chandeliers hang from them, while from the central dome is pendant a very curious brass and crystal Moorish chandelier. Another innovation is a frieze of arches, with portraits of the kings of Spain. In the four upper corners, great masses, or stalactites, or honeycomb work, richly gilded, shape the square ceiling to receive the circular dome. In this room—they tell you as you stand fairly intoxicated with the beauty and color—Charles V. was married, and the brother of Dom Pedro the Cruel, invited ostensibly to witness the tournaments, was foully murdered. It is such a vision of grace and color, the whole expression is so sweet and peaceful, so utterly removed from wars and rumors of war of the outside world, that it is extremely difficult to believe such scenes were ever enacted within its glorious embrace. Beyond is the tiny court of the Dolls, with three storeys of delicate and airy marble columns and arches and a central pretty fountain, the second storey being filled with a succession of latticed windows, and the one above forming a lovely corridor with open arches, balustrades and brilliantly colored roofs. In a long hall or dormitory, it seemed very strange to be told that the paved floor we were treading was the original of nine hundred years ago, and then, in the mosaic dado, to note an *electric button!* So the past and present jog one another, even here in lovely Spain. The dados of antique tiles and mosaics, the richly carved and gilded doors, some nine hundred and some only fifty years old, the embellishment of arches and side walls, and the glorious wealth of color, daze and confuse with their wonderful combination of grace, strength and beauty.

From these enchanted halls we turned and entered the ample gardens and pleasure-grounds attached to, and mostly enclosed by, the extensive pile. It was a fairy scene! At first we loitered upon an elevated terrace with large square pool and seats, overlooking the gardens, acres in extent, enclosed by buildings or by walls simulating façades. The air was heavy with perfume of myrtle and orange. While the gardens below were level and laid out in stiff, angular lines with box borders, cypress, orange and many flowering trees, they were so verdant and peaceful that they formed a lovely picture. Yet, just over the walls were the dusty city streets that seemed removed miles away. A staircase with wrought-iron railings draped and garlanded with lovely, tiny, cluster pink roses led to the garden below. From thence we turned into the palace to see the bath of the fair Maria de Padilla, the morganatic and beautiful wife of Dom Pedro the Cruel. It was a long vaulted apartment with an immense tank, and originally was open to the sky. The king and gentlemen of the court were accustomed to gather and look down upon the fair creature, and it was considered very gallant to drink of the water of her bath! It is said a courtier did not partake one day, and, when asked the reason, replied he " did not care for the sauce unless he could have some of the partridge!" We were just a week too late for the exuberant and riotous exhibit of roses. Their glory had departed; but numerous small flowers and shrubs, such as pomegranate and syringas, were in profuse bloom. Numerous fountains and droll water-jets, a beautiful tea-house, faced within and without with exquisite embossed tiles, and a pretty marble fish pond, statuettes and vases adorn the modern gardens, which are separated from those of Charles V. by a tall iron fence. The soft swaying of immense date palms, the cool shadows of evergreen and tropical trees, and the delicious odors of countless flowers quieted "the restless pulse of care," and made our visit a delightful one.

* * * * *

Of a very different character from the Alcazar, but equally interesting in its way, is the House of Pilate, one of the most unique sights of Seville. It is so called, because, in plan, it is a reproduction of the House of Pilate in Jerusalem. Built in the fifteenth century, for a private residence, it has been the centre of much brilliant artistic, literary and social life; has been well cared for through the ages, so that now, although unoccupied, it is most beautiful and attractive. It is the property of the Duke de Medina Celi (who he is, this deponent saith not), who rarely, if ever, visits it. So much the better probably for the travelling public. It is a fine oriental or Moorish house, with a large square patio or court, surrounded by an arcade with marble columns and spandrels, completely covered with beautiful Moorish designs in stucco, and along the corridors, rich tall dados of embossed tiles. In every corner of the court is a fine colossal, marble statue, which were added by the Duke who completed the structure at the end of ninety years, having brought them from Italy, where he lived as a viceroy of Naples. The upper gallery overlooking the court has a Gothic balustrade. The sunny court is lovely with, on one side, the Prætorium, a long fine hall with coffered ceiling of dark woods and superb, tall tile dados; upon another a small chapel with replica of the marble columns in St. Prassede in Rome, "the traditional pillar at which Christ was scourged," presented by Pius V. Upon still another is a large square room, with the same superb tiling and flat wooden roof, in which stands a copy of the table upon which the money was laid by Judas. A wide and fine staircase of stone, with side walls of solid tilings and richly panelled and carved ceiling of dark wood, leads to the upper colonnade and out upon a flat roof, one portion of which overlooks the open plaza which we crossed upon entering, which duplicates the place where our Saviour was shown to the people. High upon the walls of the buildings forming one side of this square, blazed a mass of the magenta-purple blossoms of an immense "Bougain-villa," a most gorgeous floral display. Although clinging to and covering the walls to a height of twenty or thirty feet, it threw out great branches eight and ten feet in length, which were a solid mass of flowers, waving to and fro like great silken balloons of Tyrian hue.

With the suggestive names and objects on every side filling our thoughts with and recalling vividly the incidents of the tragic story of eighteen hundred years ago, what wonder was it that, for the nonce, pretty Seville quite faded from our minds and we, in imagination and feeling, were in far-away Jerusalem, the Holy City, and when we stood in this place, and heard the words " here He was shown to the people," and this great flowering drapery of regal purple, swayed gracefully before us, that we recalled, reverently and tenderly, the words, as written by the disciple whom Jesus loved, " and they put on Him a purple robe." And Pilate saith unto them, " Behold I bring Him forth to you,"—" then came Jesus forth, wearing the crown of thorns and the purple robe."

HERE AND THERE IN SEVILLE.

The conscientious and thoughtful sight-seer who allots only a week to Seville has a busy time of it. Not that the so-called sights are so numerous, but that there are so many things one wants to see again and again, to have them clearly and indelibly impressed upon the memory.

The cathedral alone could absorb that period, for although there is no place from whence the grand and mighty structure can be viewed as an impressive whole, there is many a glimpse of window, buttress, turret or balustrade, or of all combined, that is exquisite and long to be remembered. If the interior was only free from scaffoldings and supporting beams, a week would be all too brief to fully enjoy its varied and interesting artistic and architectural features. And then the pictures within cathedral and gallery! Well! you will never be quite ready to turn away from them!

Altogether, Seville was the most delightful and spirited city we saw in Spain, being characteristic and full of life, and while not as picturesque as some other places where quaint and ruined structures abound, yet it possesses some features of interest in greater perfection and abundance. Madrid is French; Seville is Spanish! In no other place in Spain are seen so many superior houses with the beautiful semi-Moorish patios, or open courts, a most attractive and typical peculiarity, which makes even a listless stroll a succession of tasteful pictures. A passage like a porte-cochère opens, in the front façade in line with the street, directly to a central court, the end of the way being most ornamentally barred by tall wrought-iron grilles or gates. As you pass along, many a charming glimpse is had of sunny court and cozy enclosure. Some have arcades and colonnades of marble, with busts, Hermes, vases or statues; others have chairs, sofas and tables like a drawing-room, and all have a central fountain. Again, some have tall waving palms, and feathery tropical trees and a wealth of flowers. It seemed to us, from these glimpses, that there were more rocking-chairs in Seville than in all the rest of continental Europe!

One looks with interest at the yellow and muddy Guadalquivir, although its shores bear little trace of its former commercial importance, or suggestion of what it might again become with a little public spirit and enterprise. The Torre del Oro,—the Tower of Gold,—which is so pretty in the story of Seville, and such an attractive feature in the pictures, is, in these later days, a very commonplace affair. Originally a corner tower in the line of Alcazar walls or fortifications which now are swept away, it stands upon the river bank in isolated picturesqueness and forlornity. The golden tiles have disappeared. Warm orange yellow wash keeps alive the name, and at sunset absorbs a brilliant and ruddy hue. From an important position of defence it has run the gamut of a place for prisoners of state, the treasure-house of kings, the strong box where the precious gold brought by Columbus was deposited, until now, in its hoary age, it shelters the offices of a common river steamboat company. As one drives along the city streets, in an enclosure with tall iron fence is seen an imposing building over six hundred and fifty feet in length, built at an expense of over a million and a half dollars, which he is told, to his surprise (as it suggests almost every other use), is the government Tobacco and Snuff Factory. Some six thousand persons are here employed. It is one of *the* sights of Seville, but fellow-travellers reported the odors so oppressive and nauseating in that hot weather that we contented ourselves with the view from breezy carriage seats. The Palace of San Telmo, or St. Elmo, built close upon the public promenade, but with surrounding and background of lovely gardens—the home of the Montpensiers—is by far the most sumptuous and prosperous-looking structure in the city, although it has more of the appearance of an institution or barrack than a royal abode. This, however, is easily explained, for it was built originally for, and used as, a naval school. After the revolution of 1848, it was presented by ex-Queen Isabella to her sister—the Duchess of Montpensier, wife of a son of Louis Phillippe. More fortunate than the Queen, who for many years has lived an exile in France, the Duchess, now a widow, still resides in the palace, beloved by the people for her many beneficent acts and held in high esteem because of her magnificent gift to the municipality. (Died in 1897, since this was written.) We were escorted through a long suite of rooms on the ground floor which stretched one-half of the way around the Palace, all with a cozy, livable look quite unusual in such apartments. One long, spacious palatial "salon," with walls hung with paintings and portraits, and furnished with superb cabinets, vases and grand pianos, alone appeared as if not in daily use. Pretty corridors, lovely drawing-rooms with choice bric-à-brac, portraits and cozy groups of furniture, cheery bedrooms with superb hangings and draperies of satin and a multitude of portrait photographs, give the personal and characteristic appearance and expression of a home. From there we passed out upon a broad terrace with dark-blue, glossy china vases upon every post, which looked upon the indescribably beautiful gardens, with superb palms, enormous cedars, yucca trees and embowered walks in every direction. Coming from the public thoroughfare and the rich palace apartments, at once into this fresh and verdant expanse,—this atmosphere of peace,—with the cool, restful suggestion of every characteristic, was simply enchanting. Great mounds and patches of ivy, flowers without number, blossoming trees, pretty paths winding through great banks and bowers, and lovely little changing pictures, formed by the rich and varied tropical groups, were revealed with every movement. Presently, from somewhere or nowhere—for it was like magic—an overseer or gamekeeper met us. It was exquisitely droll, for with his short jacket of tan-colored cloth ornamented on the back with a great arabesque of black applique cloth, short pantaloons trimmed with wide band of red, a profusion of buttons and a fringe of leather, a large sombrero hat, and a gun, his appearance suggested one of the attachés of " Buffalo Bill." But he was very obliging and civilly took us all over the grounds (and they are of immense extent), past orange orchards, through large tracts or patches of flowers of every kind and to many a cozy and attractive nook. With evident pride and the supposition that we had never seen anything so remarkable, he conducted us to the electrical house and showed us the dynamo. Near this building was an ivy-clad tower, upon the crest of which was a stork's nest, recalling the Spanish poet's—

"—Sailing low
The broadwinged stork on the church tower top
His consecrated nest."

Father Stork was standing grimly and quietly upon one leg evidently keeping watch and ward, while Mammy Stork sat upon the old home nest. Pater and Mater familias come there every evening to visit them, and in June they all go away and do not return until February. The keeper said that the pair we saw had come there regularly for eight or ten years. Perched high in air,

The Alcazar Gardens, Seville.

so still and motionless, they present a most droll but weird and mystical appearance.

The lovely gardens and park were, until lately, upward of two miles in extent; but the Duchess has munificently presented a good one-half of them to the city for a pleasure-ground, and a wide street has been opened through, and a costly fence of stone and iron erected, and now the people have a lovely resort, while the Lady Bountiful still possesses a princely and magnificent domain. Just beyond stretches out the "Delicias," a long, spacious and imposing avenue following the course of the Guadalquivir for two miles or more, with frequent public gardens and private grounds crowded with trees, shrubs and countless brilliant flowers. It is the Central Park, the Bois de Boulogne, of Seville, and the carriages with gayly attired ladies passing up and down make, upon a pleasant late afternoon, an exceedingly animated and brilliant scene.

Expecting to see some ware purely Spanish, we drove out to the porcelain works established by the Messrs. Pickman, an English family, who now, after two generations upon the soil, carry the title of Marquis and are full-fledged Spaniards. The works occupy an old Cartuja convent in the suburbs, and might be very picturesque with a little trouble. But, regardless of effect, rude modern buildings are huddled against and around an old chapel or hall, with open roof and rose window. Two or three rooms have beautiful marqueterie ceilings and doors, and a fine apartment is finished with specimens of the decorated work. The whole process from unmixed clay to the finish is seen, but not as pleasantly as at Meissen, Derby or Sevres. A great deal of common domestic ware is made, and we saw nothing but that which could be purchased at almost any metropolitan emporium. In good order is a small chapel full of gilded carving, pictures and ecclesiastical paraphernalia and with superb choir stalls taken, we were told, from the chapel now incorporated in the works. A pleasant drive from the city, is a ruined amphitheatre and other remains, all that is left of the Roman "Italica," a city founded five hundred or more years before Christ, which was "the birthplace of three Roman Emperors, Trajan, Adrian and Theodosius." When wearied with the regular sight-seeing there was always endless entertainment in wandering through the narrow, crooked streets, with the gayest white houses dotted with green balconies and blinds, and from upper storeys the pretty " miradores," or balconies, so enclosed in glass as to appear like oriel windows, and through those lined by the little shops. Excepting an occasional lace "mantilla" gracefully worn over the head and some provincial dresses in the crowd on Corpus Christi, we saw nothing there in costume that was characteristic or national.

A Spanish poet says of Seville, "Of all the Spanish towns, is none more pretty," which voiced our sentiments as we turned reluctantly away. Conscientiously we had seen everything, remembering the old and quaint Spanish proverb, "Knowing something does not take up any room."

CORPUS CHRISTI IN SEVILLE.

If there is any one thing more than another for which the average man, woman or child will suffer, uncomplainingly, inconvenience, deprivation or utter fatigue of body and soul, it is a show, a spectacle, and especially a procession. The small boy, in face of certain penalty, will play truant that he may see the tawdry, meaningless circus come to town, while the boy of larger growth will pay a fabulous price for a balcony or window which may command a view of some passing pageant. It matters little whether it be a detachment of the Salvation Army with the inevitable musical accompaniment, the noisy parade and senseless demonstration of a political campaign, or the sightly mass or beautiful tramp of a military organization, the crowd, big and little, are sure to be there. The European tourist counts much upon witnessing the civic, military and ecclesiastical displays. Our experience was, that with the exception of the Grand Army Reviews and the great feast-day celebrations in St. Peter's in Rome, the spectacular displays, and especially the street processions, were generally incongruous, meretricious and vulgar. Yet exquisite etchings and brilliant canvas pictures can be drawn from them; for color and form, and not material, compose and are portrayed in them. We counted ourselves fortunate in being in Seville at the feast of Corpus Christi, for not only a characteristic pageant was to be seen in the narrow streets, decorations and procession, but one unique feature—not met with elsewhere in the broad world, quite worth a journey to see—the dancing before the Host in the Sagrario, or parish church, connected with the cathedral. For several days we had seen extensive preparations making, both at Seville and Granada, such as the erection along the streets and in the open plazas, of arches of imitation stone work, and also of evergreens and flowers, the raising of flag-staffs, and the setting of gayly painted masts at short distances, to uphold, on the line of the roofs, plain and colored awnings which entirely shaded the whole course of the procession and, as it finally turned out, protected the rich vestments of the ecclesiastics, the costly sacred vessels and the sumptuous coverings from passing showers. In the "Place de la Constitutione," a wide-open irregular plaza, faced by the town hall and other public edifices, the preparations were most elaborate. From windows of the hall were suspended crimson velvet hangings trimmed with gold. Along its base, great stands of five or six tiers were covered with blooming plants, between which were fine large palms. Through the centre of the Place was an avenue or passage, formed by tall scarlet staffs supporting an awning, with, at either end, a tall and really fine architectural design and arch, and upon every pole or standard heraldic shields and groups of flags. From balconies and windows upon every side, bright bits of color were injected into the scene, by gay rugs, or draperies of every kind, from damasks and satins and lace, down to bright silk patchwork coverlets. The general effect was so bright and festive, one quite forgot the character of many of the details. Some of the streets lined by the houses of the wealthy, or well-to-do classes, softly shaded by the awnings, were really beautiful, because of the sumptuous damask and glossy satin hangings. Anticipating a crowd we started at 8 A. M. for the Sagrario,—a large chapel called the parish church, connected with the cathedral,— where, upon "the octave of the Immaculate Conception" and Corpus Christi, during the service, ten boys, dressed in most dainty and picturesque costumes of pages of time of Philip III., dance upon the platform of the high altar, before the Host, or Lord, in presence of gorgeously attired cardinal, clergy and high officials of the city, a sight not to be seen anywhere else in the world. The origin of this singular custom is obscure, but it was established originally with the permission and sanction of the Pope. One legend is, that once, when the city was besieged, some boys overheard a group of soldiers talking over a plan of sudden attack. Knowing the Spanish soldiers were not on guard, they said one to another, "What can we do to let the danger be known?" One said, "Let some of us dance and divert them, while the others go and reveal the plot." So in their graceful, rollicking way, and rattling their bright castanets, they danced before the men, and the delay resulted in the safety of the city. The Sagrario, anywhere else, would be called a large church, having a long, wide nave, encircled with small chapels, and a dome over a hundred feet in height. Colossal statues and a profusion of ornamental designs, pictures and gilding crowd the interior walls. Upon this occasion, when we were so fortunate as to secure places, with unobstructed view, the walls of the choir adjacent to the high altar, were completely hidden by hangings of rich crimson velvet with bands of gold. A temporary aisle, formed by iron fences, passed through the centre to a large open space in front of the altar. To one side in this reserved space, were long gilded settees with brilliant crimson upholsterings. The high altar, which was unusually lofty, was a blaze of images and silver candelabra, with some fifty lighted candles,—a most dazzling grouping. After awhile a procession of the governor and city fathers (or their equivalent) filed in two by two, and occupied the golden settees. The "city fathers" were in evening suits and white gloves, and wore ribbons around their necks with a large golden pendant, while the old governor was resplendent with wide sash-ribbons and honors. The superb silk flag of Seville, embroidered and embossed with heraldic insignia, was borne in, in a square formed by four men in gorgeous crimson satin doublets, also embroidered with crest of the city. As they wore silken tights, and wigs that were banged in front and falling to their shoulders all around, and had hanging around their necks large-brimmed hats with long white ostrich plumes, it was decidedly theatrical, yet pretty. Men in gorgeous liveries followed with various insignia of office. There was a great deal of " backing and filling " we did not understand; some sort of service was performed at a side chapel, and then music-stands were brought in for about twenty violinists, etc. Soon appeared the procession of the Cardinal, consisting of a multitude of priests in lilac capes, lace and colored robes, followed by His Eminence in scarlet satin flowing robe with immense train carried by a bearer. After the Cardinal was seated at one side, the little boys appeared. There were ten of the little sprites, dressed most picturesquely in red and gold doublets, white satin short-clothes and white silken hose and white satin slippers, and white, red and gold hats with turned-up brims with long, snowy ostrich plumes. They took their places thoroughly unabashed, before the high altar facing one another, five upon a side. The music began, and the strange, dignified dance followed. It was most of the time a slow stately movement like a minuet: at times a quick and complete turn, and a constant changing and interlacing of positions very like calisthenics, accompanied by the singing of the boys and clicking of their castanets. They danced with their hats on before the Host, which is regarded as a great privilege. It was certainly extremely pretty and artistic, for their whitehosed legs and dainty bowed-slippers added much to the grace of it, and the effect of the rich costumes was decidedly picturesque. It seemed incongruous in a church, yet it was in perfect keeping with the theatrical surroundings. The dance ceased. The little fellows dropped for a moment upon their knees and then descended the two or three steps of the altar, to the open space before the group of city officials, and were soon at it again.

While they were dancing in this space, twelve men in white and black robes filed in, each carrying a huge silver censer, and proceeded to " cense " or fumigate the whole concern. Ere long thick clouds of incense smoke dimmed the view of the high altar, and all the while the little fellows, like fairies or sprites, were moving to and fro in measured step. Then they passed down the aisle (not very reverently, for they were full of mischief), followed by the glowing scarlet Cardinal, the ecclesiastics and the civic officials, and the service was ended. It is repeated for two or three days, twice a day, but without the attendance of the city authorities. Upon the occasion of the fête of the Immaculate Conception, the costumes are blue and white instead of crimson and white. We witnessed the service again, with the Cardinal kneeling, as in profound prayer, and upon one side the Duchess of Montpensier, a King's daughter in heavy mourning, kneeling in continuous devotion at a "prie-dieu" upon the opposite side with several of her family around her. It gained in impressiveness by the absence of the city fathers, but was spectacular and theatrical to the last.

At the close of the first service we hurried out and made our way through a dense crowd, being assisted and treated with marked attention and courtesy, to the " Place de la Constitutione," where from a delightful balcony, we overlooked the whole processional display. Upon this day all the treasures of the cathedral, many of which we had seen, comprising temples, statues, candelabra, huge structures for holding the Host, all in solid silver, with rich jewels, costly robes of satin, gold and velvet, are carried upon the platforms so draped with the golden and colored brocades as to hide the carriers beneath, from the cathedral to the church of St. Saviour in solemn procession, followed by the ecclesiastics and officials in their rich robes and insignia. Before the church the dance is given again, and then the procession makes a circuit of the city and returns to the cathedral. The scene, the general effect, from our balcony, while theatrical and showy, was very brilliant and beautiful. Two lines of mounted soldiers lining one side of the plaza, while every window and balcony was a glory of kaleidoscopic color, formed a regular Joseph's coat, from a satin damask bedspread to a patchwork quilt. Every platform with a costly silver candelabra and paraphernalia was profusely decorated with flowers and numerous burning candles. As the great "Custodia," a tall temple or pagoda-like structure containing the Host passed, the effect was fine and impressive. The flash of sunlight upon the silver temple, and the purple capes and white lace of the ecclesiastics, the golden vestments and the gorgeous scarlet robes and train of the Cardinal, was most striking. The group of carriers in crimson satin, with the flag of Seville, was followed by the Captain General and city officials, each with a liveried servant to carry his hat! The procession first rounded a corner beneath us, then gradually curved to one of the arches in the plaza, defiled through the aisle formed by flagstaffs, festoons of gas jets and flowers, and passed out of sight through the distant arch. As the Host, Corpus Christi—the body of Christ—rested in the centre of the plaza, the incense-bearers, enveloped it in a cloud of smoke. Just as the last end of the procession disappeared there was a patter of rain which soon developed into a heavy shower. Then the cavalry, upon spirited horses, who had stood so still the whole length of the plaza in two or three rows, slowly formed and passed splendidly through the arch, and the pageant for us was over. The day was to terminate with a grand bull-fight, but it rained so heavily the ring was unfit, and at three o'clock official notice was given that there would be none. Thousands were disappointed, but we were glad of it, for, with a popular writer, "our sympathies were with the bull." Every town of any importance has its ring. It is the national sport. "Did you not see a bull-fight?" some one will ask! No! for with an aversion to the sight of blood, that makes a common butcher's stall far from agreeable, it seemed hardly worth while to so mar a pleasure-trip. Almost every one we met who had witnessed one said, "Don't go," and yet, it was noticeable the majority went more than once. Strangely incongruous it seems, that a day given up in honor of the body of Christ should close with the brutal slaughter of helpless animals and the endangering of human lives, with the applause of countless thousands, fearfully suggestive in spirit of the bloodthirsty cry of the multitude of old, "Crucify Him! Crucify Him!"

17

WITH MURILLO IN SEVILLE.

FAMILIARITY with the masterpieces scattered through the galleries and palaces of continental Europe had long ago inspired a genuine love and enthusiastic admiration for the works of Murillo, that strange artist, who, in his choice of subjects, whether realistic or mystical, matter of fact or deeply spiritual, seems equally at home. Somewhere, years ago, we read, "Until you have seen his works in Spain, you will not know what a Murillo is." This alone was sufficient to create a longing to visit that romantic country which is fast becoming the happy hunting-ground of the latter-day tourist. But after seeing the wonderful galaxy in Seville, of the superb group at the Gallery, the gems at the Cathedral and the fine duo at the Hospital of La Caridad, and later the marvellous canvasses in the Royal Gallery and Academy of San Fernando at Madrid and recalling the lovely Holy Child in the National at London, the dreamy, mystical Immaculate Conception in the Louvre at Paris, the irresistible fascinating "gamins" at Munich, the incomparable St. John at Vienna and the same and other subjects in the Hermitage at St. Petersburg,— we questioned seriously the correctness of the assertion. There are ways of looking at pictures, and again there are ways. Sometimes, as we have listened to the comments of critics, artists and connoisseurs, we have wondered just where their enjoyment of the pictures themselves comes in! For ourselves, we were content to give up entirely to the soft glory of rich and liquid coloring,—the deep, mystical, dreamy sentiment and the wonderful, suggestive expression, ignoring possible flecks and flaws and imperfections as something life, or at any rate our sojourn in Spain, was too brief for,—and relegating all such to the conscientious student and the heartless critic. The view, from the standpoint of enjoyment, may be that of ignorance, but to many it is preferable to everlasting fault-finding under the affected guise of cultivation and intelligence. The pictures which form the Gallery at Seville, hang not in sumptuous or well-ordered "salons," as in continental cities, but upon the dull terracotta walls of the old disused church or chapel of the ancient Convent de la Merced, in the very heart of the city, founded way back in the twelfth century, but suppressed in 1835. With a barrel-vaulted roof covered with indifferent and gaudy frescoes, a dome rising above the intersection of single nave and transept, pictures framed in wide, plain mouldings with gilding decidedly the worse for age and wear, the paintings themselves looking hard and dry, and a general appearance of dinginess and forlornity, it is not an ideal gallery. The dozen and a half paintings by Murillo are like jewels in an ash-heap. One sees also two fine cloistered courts and a museum of unsightly, although doubtless interesting, fragments from Italica, the old Roman stronghold in the far suburbs of the city. But there is a peculiar satisfaction in seeing the priceless gems of an age that is past sumptuously and richly housed. The majority of the Murillos were painted for a single Capuchin convent. Some look as if fading, but the majority are warm and rich in coloring and grand and powerful in sentiment and purpose. There are several " Immaculate Conceptions" which confirm the feeling that he painted this subject, until, at last, in the one taken by Soult and now in the Louvre, he realized his ideal. None approach it in beauty, dreamy sentiment or soft liquid coloring. In a line upon one side hang a dozen or more large canvasses—made a joy forever by his magic touch. The one, considered the finest and said to have been regarded by Murillo as his best, is St. Thomas of Villaneuva giving alms. The old Bishop, in full black robes, stands at a Cathedral door distributing gifts to a promiscuous crowd. Fine opportunity is given for a great variety of attitude, expression and coloring. The figure of a kneeling beggar is very fine, while a little group in one corner of a mother and child looking at a piece of money bestowed, is a picture of itself. A large picture represents St. Joseph with his arm around the child Jesus. The lovely figure and sweet innocent face of the child recalls that in the London Gallery, the position and dress being similar. One could sit for hours before this one dear little face and form alone.

The Celebrated "Virgin of the Napkin" (so called because painted upon a serviette for the cook of a convent) is small, but very brilliant, yet soft and delicious in coloring. But it seemed to us nothing could exceed in pathos, deep interest or spirituality and rich glowing representation the Vision of St. Francis of Assisi and the St. Anthony of Padua, which hang side by side, the first holding in his loving embrace the Saviour dead,—the other the Infant and living Christ.

In the former, the dead Christ suspended upon the cross has miraculously loosed one hand and returns the loving, tender embrace of St. Francis, who looks up into the Redeemer's face with a yearning gaze full of passionate love, reverential awe and sublime pity. The world represented by a ball or sphere rolls away from his feet, while two lovely cherubs hold an open book in the air.

In the latter the Saint is kneeling with a lily in one hand and with head reposing lovingly against the Divine Child. The radiant, ecstatic and satisfied expression of the purified face and gentle eyes is marvellous, but the child is only a lovely, fair and handsome babe that might be called by any name. The flesh tint of the plump little limbs and form is very beautiful. Above is a little glory of cherubs, which Murillo knew so well how to group and paint. Some authorities consider this picture even finer than the one of the same name in the Cathedral. It has the freshness of the physique of untried youth, the ecstasy and sentimental bliss of inexperience, the simple joy, delight and satisfaction of the present. It asks no more, it possesses the realization of its dream, for the mortal arms embrace the Infant Christ—and satisfaction and content are supreme.

The other evidences mature and impressive forgetfulness of self in the reverent yearning tenderness and pity with which the Saint farther advanced in life and experience looks up at his crucified Lord, and, in the calm, earnest realization that a life has been laid down for him, would fain do something for Him in return. Both faces are wonderful; both hold one with an irresistible power and spell. In the hallowing, quieting atmosphere of these wondrous creations one forgets everything but the grand, sublime fact of a Saviour born and crucified and ever living to make intercession for us. One cannot wander through Europe and look without increasing interest and unfailing delight at the works of the Old Masters, without being impressed with the magnitude of the debt which art lovers owe to the Romish church, in that so many of the masterpieces were painted originally for votive offerings, gifts or decorations for her altars, sacred edifices and conventual buildings. Through long years of tumult, of wars and rumors of wars, that, which in private possession would doubtless have been destroyed, has been conserved in her dim sanctuaries and sacred retreats, and the art world is infinitely richer and fuller to-day, for her unconscious guardianship. One wonders sometimes if the demand were the same to-day, whether the supply would be proportionately fine! For the high water mark has apparently been reached in painting, sculpture and architecture. But the intelligent response of to-day would certainly not be marked by such droll incongruities. The Madonna would not be simply the woman of the artist's country with her infant child, which is such a marked characteristic of the Old Masters, but a typical Jewish maiden, the " handmaid of the Lord," with the draperies and environment of the Holy Land or Orient, and the donor of a picture nowadays would scarcely consent to being complacently included in a group of those who lived some eighteen hundred years ago.

Near the yellow Guadalquivir is the old church and convent "De La Caridad," a visit to which one would be sorry to lose, for, upon the crimson damask walls of its exceedingly narrow chapel, hangs Murillo's wonderful picture of "Moses Smiting the Rock." It is a very long, narrow canvas, richly framed, but hung too high for comfortable examination. Unfortunately for us, the light upon it was such a glare that it was quite impossible to see the entire picture at once. The central figure of Moses is the least

satisfactory of all, being theatrical and studied.
The rest is simplicity itself, a great crowd of
thirsty ones made glad and exultant by the miraculous bringing forth of the refreshing stream.
The faces are so famished and eager, so exultant
and grateful! At one side upon a white horse
is a child, quite suggestive of his famous beggar
boys, laughing for joy. Beside is a young girl
upholding a jug which is a complete and exquisite picture of itself. A dear little baby held
in its mother's arm is trying to get a drink of the
life-giving flood. To the other side a dog is seen
lapping, lapping, with as much evident delight
and joy as any human being, while a child close
by drinks eagerly from a dish. The story is
simply but dramatically told and the whole picture is a mass of richest tones and tints,—of
glowing and brilliant colors. Yet for this wonderful composition Murillo received but six hundred and fifty dollars! and perhaps he never
collected the whole of that! Compared with
this think of the prices of to-day! Five
other pictures by Murillo, one "The Feeding of
the Multitude," a large canvas much praised by
the authorities, grace the walls and make this
little boudoir of a chapel a painter's shrine. The
group of buildings composed of chapel, convent

and hospital enclose two open, quiet, sunlit courts, bright with flowers and shrubs. Hundreds of years ago a gay and dissolute courtier turned over a new leaf and brought forth fruits meet for repentance in the erection and rich endowment of this pile, wherein even to-day " a multitude of impotent folk," aged and decrepit men, find a peaceful harbor until the storms are o'er, cared for by a devoted band of Sisters or nuns, who in their blue gray habits and picturesque starched head-gear flit to and fro in their quiet ministrations in an atmosphere of peace and retirement in strange contrast with the life at their very gates. So history repeats itself. Out of the bitter hath come forth the sweet! Again, as of old, where sin abounded grace doth much more abound, in this ceaseless ministration, this perpetual benediction of peace on earth and good will toward men.

THE PRIDE OF CORDOVA.

The keen regret with which we left Seville, catching a last glimpse of the summit of the stately Giralda, above a thicket of trees as we turned away, was quickly (so fickle is the effect of continuous travel) merged and lost in delightful anticipation and pleasant curiosity, for we realized that our faces were set toward fresh fields, even Cordova and her famous Cathedral Mosque only four short hours away. Perhaps the scenery and country all that warm and lovely morning could truthfully be called a little tame, and certainly would seem monotonous and wearisome were we compelled to pass that way frequently, but we were so comfortable in a compartment all by ourselves, which in this land of the omnipresent and perpetually burning cigarette is an inestimable boon, and were in such a receptive mood we enjoyed every rod. At times we looked over fertile, undulating meadows to the low lying hills bounding the horizon; again we passed over level plains yellow with harvested fields; past great hedgerows of gray aloes and enormous prickly pears in full bloom, extensive olive plantations and miles of country, literally without a tree. Spain is properly called a "treeless land" in the sense of almost entire absence of forest growth or trees of any great size or age. Being in a cheerful frame, we were much entertained by characteristic trifles along the route; gentlemen at the way stations with picturesque sombreros and queer little ornamented jackets such as schoolboys used to wear; the ringing of a common country dinner bell as signal for starting of the train; an occasional costume and the numbers of beautiful children and fresh, handsome women. There was something droll in the sight of plants and flowers we cultivate carefully in pots, growing to a height of eight or ten feet in open air. Just out of Seville we passed a large patch or thicket of pomegranate bushes, starred with the same brilliant scarlet flowers we value so highly, growing as rank as pestilent weeds. Here and there low country houses with tiled roofs and side walls dazzling with frequent whitewash, and occasionally, upon an elevation, the ruin of some old tower or castle wall, give a touch of life to the scene. In thinking of Cordova we found we dwelt only upon the wonderful Mosque, and immediately upon arrival were much surprised to find it so lively, for even the guide-book spoke of it as "dead." On our way to the hotel we passed beautiful public gardens, pretty squares and many fine houses. After lunch we picked our way through the old narrow and crooked streets of the town, stopping frequently to look at the charming patios or courts, visible through a vestibule with handsome iron gates and often a blaze of color from numerous flowering plants, until we came in a tremor of excitement and delight to the ancient Moorish Mosque now called the Cathedral. As with the Alhambra, the exterior presents little to attract, for, as a matter of fact, as one approaches he sees only great heavy walls with massive buttresses and fancy battlements, more suggestive of a fortress of defensive structure than of a church or ecclesiastical pile. Yet with the multitude of towers, the variety of battlements and the architectural traces of former entrances, it is impressive and picturesque. A tall massive tower with a number of bells replaces the original tower of the muezzins and forms the chief entrance to the famous Court of the Oranges and thence to the Mosque itself. It is a perfect transformation to step

The Mosque, Cordova.

from the city street into this Court some four hundred and thirty feet long and two hundred and ten wide, full of shining orange trees, plashing fountains, groups of beggars, soldiers with scarlet trousers, and frequently women in black enveloped in the lovely and graceful Spanish lace mantillas or veils. Originally stately palms and sombre cypresses also adorned it, but a hurricane made sad havoc seventy or more years ago with them, and Spanish indolence has prevented a replacing. Colonnades of marble columns and arches remain—all a little worse for wear. Crossing this open space, to the great elaborately carved doors of the Cathedral proper, we lifted aside the heavy greasy leathern curtain, and in an instant passed from the open sunlit court into a scene so strange, weird and novel that it seems well-nigh indescribable. Everywhere color of soft red, blue and cream, lifted in double arches in the air; a forest of marble columns of pink and gray and white stretching away and, with the supported arches, losing themselves in the soft haze of distance. The form, which at first does not impress one, is square, with twenty-nine naves or aisles from north to south and nineteen from east to west, all lined and designated by these beautiful columns, wreathed with the soft glory of the ruddy and snowy arches. Alas! it is *low*, the ceiling being only thirty-five feet above the ancient pavement, which inspires the feeling that you must be in a magnificent crypt and wonder what superb architectural marvel towers above it. But it is considered "the finest type in Europe of the true temple of Islam." Since those halcyon days we have looked upon the Mosque at Damascus, now in ruins, and the famous Acksah of Jerusalem, but the memory of that weird and matchless interior suffers no loss. At first, the sight of the forest of columns and the maze of arches is bewildering,—the effect kaleidoscopic and bewitching. With every change of position the scene varies. It seems to move! It is confusing, but ere long, as the eye becomes accustomed to it, it becomes orderly, serene and sublime. Here and there through lengthened vistas of delicious beauty, appears far away the exquisite fretwork and intricate designs of the Moorish style. Sometimes one looks down through a long vista of orderly arches, then, perchance, diagonally through a confusion or chaos of arches and colors to the soft gleaming of distant buff and red or to some remote sunlit arch, gilded and glowing. It is not "churchly" ecclesiastical, in the sense that Westminster,

Notre Dame, St. Stephen's or even St Peter's are. It is as tranquil and pensive as a place for the dead, yet it is also as sensuous and voluptuous as a bath! It is too low to inspire awe, but it animates enjoyment and admiration unceasingly. It is a soothing and tranquillizing monotone of mellow, oriental, voluptuous beauty which intoxicates the sense and bewilders the mind. It conduces to sentimental dreaming and to meditative thought as well, but it does not uplift and support as the grand, lofty old Gothic naves do. It is a dream, a vision, a fairy scene, not spectacular, sensational or dramatic, but soft, solemn and satisfying. It reminds, at times, of a military drill, so statuesque, and then again so full of rhythmic and stately movement does the forest of slender shafts and columns appear. As you move, scarcely knowing where to begin, and uncertain as to where the ethereal mirage may end, you may perchance look down some apparently interminable vista of delicate, mellow-tinted arches and see at the end an iron lattice, or grille, with slants of golden sunshine streaming through. No matter which way your enraptured vision may turn, always are visible the dainty, delicate-hued arches, the slender columns of jasper, porphyry and marble of innumerable tints. You may sit for hours and not a movement or a sound will break the calm repose, and then perhaps some black-robed figure will glide quietly by, or kneel at some distant shrine; or a company of acolytes in scarlet robes and white lace will saunter along laughingly, or the sweet tones of the organ reverberate gently through the solemn place. It is easy to say there are from one thousand to twelve hundred columns, or were originally ; that there are rows of twenty-nine arches one way and nineteen the other, intersecting at right angles, but this carries no impression or idea of its witchery and fascination. If this unique structure could only have been left unchanged and unharmed, it would now be one of the architectural Meccas of the world. Completed in 796 it stood, a dream of loveliness, with arches studded with emeralds and rubies, with walls perforated and incised in delicate lace-like conceits, and roof glistening with color and gold, in which the Moslem made his graceful and picturesque obeisance for hundreds of years, and then the incoming and capturing Christians "purified" it, and in 1521 ruthlessly tore away columns and arches and decorations, making a great open space in the centre, in which they built a Cathedral which anywhere else would be imposing and fine, but here is grotesque and inharmonious. It

Cordova Cathedral, Court of Oranges.

is said that Charles V., who had given permission but was unaware of what was being done, indignantly declared, "You have built here that which can be built anywhere else, but you have destroyed that which was unique in the world." Yet he tore out the heart of the Alhambra for his palace! How difficult to see ourselves as others see us! Within this church, so utterly at variance with the style and spirit of the old Mosque, is a magnificent Choir, with superb carved stalls of dark mahogany and in framing of all sorts of graceful conceits a double row of carved New and Old Testament scenes of wonderful beauty. Close to the church is an interesting room, the exquisite ornamentation of whose walls has been discovered within only a few years. It is now supposed to be the place where the Koran was kept. At the rear of the Mosque is a room where, until this last was discovered, was supposed to be the receptacle of the Koran. It is such a gem of architecture and art, such a fitting place for holy books, that it is a pity the question was ever raised. It is a square chapel with a dome completely encrusted with soft, yet richly colored, mosaics. No jewel could be more exquisitely embedded, no setting more richly wrought. A small chapel opens from it with a doorway decorated with mosaics, having all the soft richness of an India shawl and a ceiling formed of a single block of marble sculptured in shape of a shell! Could anything in solid stone be more poetical? The whole structure sets at defiance all ordinary power or manner of description. Almost all ecclesiastical buildings, with their spacious naves, transepts and shadowy aisles, impart some one distinct impression or idea, and if confusion reigns below, the lofty roofs tell a story of form and comeliness. But this is simply a square space with

"A portal and an altar everywhere."

with, along its sides, a row of dark inharmonious modern chapels and, but for the hideous vandalism of building a modern church in the centre, would be in design a checker-board formed by multitudinous aisles crossing at right angles. The lack of height dwarfs its possible expression and deprives it of grandeur. But the wilderness of lovely arches and exquisite columns, the witchery of the vistas, the play of light from numerous cupolas and the predominating air of quiet and repose, make it unusually beautiful and attractive.

"Seven hundred years ago
Moslem made this structure grow."

Is it "Nemesis" that this pride of the haughty Moor which occupies the site of a destroyed church has in turn had its very heart torn from it to do reverence to the religion it despised?

GOLDEN HOURS AT CORDOVA AND ARANJUEZ.

Cordova may possess a multitude of features of interest, but a sudden and unexpected change in our plans and itinerary, which involved immediate curtailment of the length of our sojourn, obliged us to content ourselves with our never-to-be-forgotten tarry and reverie in the old Cathedral Mosque; a walk to the ancient Roman bridge, a tower of strength even to-day, which with several stone arches spans the rapid and muddy Guadalquivir, and an evening visit to the annual fair or sale,—a most characteristic, picturesque and interesting scene. A large open promenade adjoining the public gardens was brilliantly and fancifully illuminated, and along the whole length upon either side were little gayly decorated booths, crowded with toys, lamps, jewelry, confectionery and household wares, tended in many cases by persons in provincial costumes. Games of chance, and many a booth with cauldron of boiling fat in which quite toothsome-looking cakes were frying, and numberless devices to wheedle the " pesetas " from the lookers-on, were in full blast. At intervals among the trees were beautiful, circular, raised platforms with ornamental, tented canopies, which belonged to various clubs, where every evening was music and dancing to the wee small hours. The motley crowd was quite as interesting as the fair. Our last morning we devoted to nature, as illustrated by the " Huerto de los Arcos," the suburban estate and garden of the Marquis de la Niga de Armijo." The road from the city stretches out for three miles in a white, straight line, leading uphill all the way. But it was a charming drive, for it was through the open country; the air was fresh and sweet and a procession of wild flowers attended us all the way. An aureole of yellow, pink, blue, red and purple fairly surrounded us. As for the scarlet poppies, they were everywhere! Along the roadsides in great nodding plumes, in the yellow grain fields, and in some places well-nigh dominating the spontaneous growth upon the hillsides, blazed the rich masses of glowing scarlet. And all along were pensive, meditative and solemn olive groves! What more could we ask? Over us, "like God's great pity," blue sky and great floating white clouds ; around us, color and soft verdancy; before us the rising ridge upon which we could discern the little Moorish villa and the terraced gardens we were to visit, and on every side lovely views over undulating hills and green billowy fields, and within!—well! the consciousness that we were in sunny Spain when it was sunny and just the right time,—was not the least of our pleasant emotions! At the end of the road an attendant opened an iron gate and ushered us into fairyland; a succession of terraces upon the steep hillside with a thicket of orange trees bowed down with golden fruit; pomegranates, brilliant with scarlet blossoms, and roses and and roses without number. Sometimes great, high walls which upheld a terrace were vine-clad and flower-decked as if arranged only for a temporary or festive occasion. Gradually the zigzag walk took us to a little elevated platform or terrace upon which stood the villa—the only residence upon the place. It was but one lofty story in height. We stepped at once into a Moorish hall or sitting-room in the centre, from which opened upon the terrace three arched doorways, commanding an extensive view. Adjoining was a dainty billiard-room with tiny Moorish buffets and queer little racks filled with handsome placques. There may have been three small sleeping-rooms and,—that was all! For so large an estate and so fine a garden it seemed, compared with our way of living, infinitesimally small. But we were told the Spanish people do not like the isolated life and never entertain in the country, and are very simple in their tastes. Upon the plateau, well shaded and overlooking much that is beautiful, were small tables where early coffee and the midday meal are frequently taken. The view from the villa is magnificent. One seems lifted high in air! Way down in the depths lies, like a great green and brown placque, the olive-dotted, charming valley or plain; to the right, gently rising hills with scarcely a tree. Cordova, with a bit of the yellow Guadalquivir lying slumbering like a true Spanish peasant in the sun upon the plain, while to the left the hills are bolder and fade away in great purple, shadowy slopes. The profuse display of our common garden flowers as well as many we nurture in conservatories was amazing. Arbutilons, pomegranates and numerous other plants stand loaded with blossoms, to a height of eight or ten feet. Along the slope of one walk upon the walls were one hundred pots of blooming carnations; along another a great bridal troupe of Annunciation lilies, while fragrant masses of white and yellow jasmine waved to and fro on every side. An old Moorish quarry—which otherwise would have been an eyesore—has been beautifully utilized, the rough banks being festooned and covered with ivy and roses and the bed levelled, and upon it, picked out with tiny borders of box, the family coat-of-arms. All this goes on from year to year, for frost is unknown—and the place is kept fresh and vigorous by irrigation. When the atmosphere is perfectly clear, the distant snowy peaks of the Sierras beyond Granada can be discerned, but that day they were more like faint, indistinct banks of summer cloud. With the wonderful view ever unfolded, and the hillside below so rich with verdure of orange trees, and the air so fragrant with perfume of their blossoms and of countless roses, it will be readily understood why two brief hours seemed very short indeed. Early in the afternoon we took the unavoidable, because only, train northward, which was to give us our first experience of Spanish night travel. Throughout the afternoon our way laid through a richly cultivated country, with, as before, scarcely a tree for miles, until late in the day, when we came into a most varied and hilly country, apparently arid and desolate, and in sight of a fine chain of bold and picturesque mountains. The evening closed in upon us. There was no "sleeper." We could do nothing but sit bolt upright, be uncomfortable, think what a slow country Spain is, and doze when we could. In the afternoon we had four men in our compartment, smoking continuously of course, and were in despair as we thought of the coming night watches, but one after another they disappeared, and at midnight what was left of us was in full possession. Like the French after Magenta, one more such victory would have exhausted us! We left the train at Aranjuez at four-fifteen the next morning. At that hour it was so still, the air so deliciously refreshing, and the whole place so much more embowered in trees than any town we had seen, that to us, tired, sleepy and hungry, it was simply delightful. As we drove to the hotel we caught beautiful glimpses of the palace, long, low arcades, church domes, lovely gardens and stately avenues. The wretched little inn was very crowded because of the bull-fights and races. The servants, who lodge out, had not appeared, the tables were bare, and everything far from attractive. But as the day wore on and the various paraphernalia appeared it was more habitable, and we were fairly comfortable. A few hours later we started to see the gardens and palace. Way back in the fifteenth century some illustrious Order planted trees, erected a villa and commenced laying out the gardens. Later it became the property of the crown, and after many vicissitudes the present palace and lovely gardens have been created and developed. For a long time the residence of the court, it looks even now like another Versailles. As it is rarely occupied or used at the present day it has a neglected and shabby look which is pitiful, which is to be regretted, for the trees with the growth of centuries are so fine and the gardens so lovely. The junction of the Tagus and the Xarama forms an island upon which the large palace stands. Along one side sweeps the wide and rapid Tagus, while all around is a moat filled with a rushing stream. The river adds much to the charm, for along the parterre is a wall of stone with rail and row of vases, over which one looks down upon the rushing waters, as they break in a long cascade, to the channel below. The parterre lies to one side, and is overlooked from the palace, and is level, with meandering walks, stiff flower-beds, roses by the thousand, and sweet-williams, canterbury bells, larkspurs, and many other old-fashioned flowers, in wildest profusion. It is a brilliant scene, this mosaic of floral colors, with here and there a white statuette or pretty fountain. To and fro we strolled in the hot sunshine, wild with delight; for whether "in it," or above it, as from palace windows, or looking across it, it was like stained glass, a mass of rich, deep, glowing colors. A little bridge with statues on either side leads to the larger enchanting and extensive park-like gardens. Lovely, shadowy avenues of palm trees stretch along the river terrace. Miles of hedge-lined walls radiate in every direction. Through the thickets of living green gleam the white of inferior statuary or the brilliant colors of rose trees or flowering shrubs. Huge trees wave their branches and cast cool shadows, and one may walk all day and scarcely repeat a path. It is stiff and angular, but none the less lovely, with the numberless cool, green, shadowy vistas to charm the eye and quiet the spirit. We walked through a multitude of rooms in the palace, all richly papered, or with drapings of silk and satin, many pieces of quaint and antique furniture, and a large collection of mantel clocks—the fad of a king. The only remarkable room is the "Capo di Monte," a conceit and extravagance of Charles III., a large corner "salon" with walls and domed ceiling entirely faced with china slabs or tiles. Upon a white, glossy ground appear varied Japanese or Chinese figures, trees, vines and flowers, all brilliantly colored, and, although put up in 1762, as fresh as new. It is curious and interesting, but is in questionable taste. Later in the day we visited the "Gardens del Principe," laid out upon a bolder and broader plan, with wide avenues of stately trees, little lakes, streams, summer-houses and spaces with serpentine and meandering walks. The island gardens are contracted and villa-like, but this is park-like. Within its enclosure is a miniature palace, a sort of Trianon, called "Casa del Labrador," or workman's cottage, an affectation, for money could hardly do more, although taste could do better with less. It is a long, low structure, with projecting wings at either end, forming a three-sided court, with exterior profusely embellished with statues and busts. Within, leading to the state apartments, is a staircase, upon which fifteen thousand dollars of gold has been used. A suite of small rooms is shown, richly hung with superb silks and damasks. Two or three are completely covered with exquisitely embroidered silk, one with hand-embroidered scenes, while the woodwork of several is delicately inlaid with pearl and silver. One tiny boudoir is finished in mahogany ornamented with gold and platina, at a cost of twenty thousand dollars! Gorgeous clocks of all kinds and sizes, exquisite china, and much indifferent statuary are scattered lavishly through the rooms. It is a relief to be out in the air and under the grand old trees again. Deserted by the court, and rarely visited, this Spanish Fontainebleau, with its stately park and lovely gardens, lies fallow and unused year after year. Meanwhile the overburdened people are hopelessly crushed by taxation, the rich natural resources of the country are undeveloped, and the regal heritage of a long line of kings seems perilously near utter bankruptcy.

TOLEDO,

"THE CROWN OF SPAIN."

Perhaps we enjoyed the approach to Toledo the more, because, with the exception of the Alhambra, it was the first place we had seen upon an elevation. It certainly, that bright sunny morning, was very fine, for "the crown of Spain" is a city set upon a hill. Miles away, across the verdant valley, the ancient battlemented walls and towers and the dominating pile of the great Alcazar, crowning the summit of an abrupt eminence with cheerless environment of treeless hills, brown and scantily covered, stood out like a picture, clear, bold and flashing in the sunlight. It was a railway journey from Aranjuez of no particular interest, of a little more than two hours. The station is upon the plain at the base of the hill, which is fortunate, for the rapidly ascending drive is peculiarly imposing and striking, for the situation upon the hill crest is so unique, with bluff-like sides, and a deep almost encircling gorge or ravine through which flows rapidly the yellow Tagus, while the opposing banks rise wild and sombre, and the valley by which we came spreads out below, fresh and verdant with the river winding ribbon-like out of sight. As we climbed the hill, the gray, square, four-towered Alcazar seemed like a mighty fortress, bidding defiance to any intruder, —the battlemented walls gave the brown roofs, towers and cupolas of the city a fortified and well protected appearance. Across the ravine and river a fine stone-arched bridge fairly leaps, the smooth beautiful road zigzags upward past walls and terraces commanding superb views, to the level of the city, while at the entrance towers and gates confront with a decidedly formidable and belligerent effect. The number of really good hotels in Spain is so infinitesimal that it is a kindness to record that here, beautifully located, in this antiquated city, has been built within a few years a fine structure, Moorish in general style, with all the appointments and requirements of the present day. It commands a lovely view, and at the time of our visit was admirably conducted. The town is a labyrinth of narrow streets, so tortuous and often turning so abruptly, that it is easy to lose one's way. It was probably so built to afford shade and coolness in the torrid summers, and in times of war and conflict to make it easier of defence. On every side are melancholy traces of former richness and grandeur in the ornamented doors, iron grilles, balconies, heraldic designs in stone and exuberantly sculptured stonework. But it has a pitiful, hopeless and disheartened expression, although the restoration of the Alcazar, the erection of the town hall, the new hotel and other buildings, suggest something more than a flickering vitality. But its old-time glory has departed. Its churches are dismantled and ruined; its palaces fallen into "innocuous desuetude." Perhaps though, it is better for the race, for the Spain of the future, that "Ichabod" is written so plainly upon it. As its streets are too narrow for two vehicles to pass one another, the din and noise of the signals or warnings from the various corners is sometimes terrific. One is kept on the "qui vive" the whole time, for there is something picturesque, interesting or amusing upon every side. It may be the street is a vista of color and floral decorations because of the oft repeated balconies being filled to overflowing with potted plants in profuse bloom, or perchance in some secluded and quiet turn a young soldier with scarlet trousers is seen with upturned eyes talking softly to a young

Toledo Cathedral Choir.

girl behind the small, quaint iron grating of a window, tritely suggesting a nineteenth-century Romeo and Juliet. While carelessly noting the droll yet picturesque incongruities of ancient affluence and present squalor upon every side, a sudden turning revealed a vista of irregular houses with a multitude of dark and shadowy balconies with, at the end, peering into the blue sky and flooded with sunlight, the great tower and spire of the celebrated Cathedral. The exterior is disappointing, being a medley of styles, but the west front, with its decoration of statues, floriated ornaments and sculpturings, is extremely interesting and picturesque. Way up above the entrance porch, sculptured in stone, is the scene of the Last Supper—the figures being seen behind a table which also constitutes a cornice in front! It is folly to expect to see a Spanish Cathedral as a unique whole, for they are almost invariably crowded or hugged or half obscured by inferior and insignificant buildings. An open plaza here affords ever a fine view of the west front and an attending highly ornamented recessed court,—open Gothic work,—elegant cupola, and the bell tower some three hundred and twenty-nine feet in height, with fanciful termination of iron rays, cross, etc. Upon the opposite side is a spacious and magnificent court faced on every side by superb, lofty Gothic cloisters. But the interior overwhelms, with its vast extent, its opulent details of form and color and its solemn and impressive air. Five mighty and majestic naves (of graduated heights) stretch away in the solemn shadows and dim religious light a distance of more than four hundred feet. The grand central one, whose uplifted roof seems like a firmament, is blocked, as in most of the Spanish Cathedrals, with the Choir, a solid structure with outer walls, a mass of exquisite arches, delicate marble columns and sumptuous carvings, yet high above and beyond it are seen the apsidal end, the odd gilded and colored retablo—of the high altar. Looking down the other naves, one sees a row of chapels encircling with peculiarly beautiful effect the apse, with richly carved marble screens of floriated Gothic design and huge gates of iron and gold, and everywhere like choicest jewels and precious stones, the glorious color and sheen of seven hundred and fifty superb, ancient, stained-glass windows. The great supporting columns rise in unbroken lines —a miniature forest—and bend together in the vaulted roof like graceful and stately palms. As for six long centuries all that wealth and intelligent taste could do was wrought by hundreds of artists, there is a bewildering yet strangely harmonious amount of ornamentation. The details of the choir are peculiarly beautiful —having five carved wooden stalls with columns of delicately tinted marbles, supporting alabaster canopies! It being Corpus Christi week, the altar frontals were of superb ancient embroidery in daintiest designs and delicate colors. Between the deep chapel, in which stands the high altar before a tall retablo or reredos, gorgeous with scenes and figures carved in wood and gaudily colored and gilded, and two costly ormolu pulpits upon marble standards made out of the tombs of a discarded favorite, and the choir, are a lofty screen and gates of ingeniously wrought iron. For Corpus Christi week only, behind the altar were hung the tent-cloths of *our* Queen Isabella, formed of great squares or blocks of cloth of gold enriched with crests and heraldic insignia. The walls which enclose this chapel display exquisite screen work in marble, in Gothic designs, surmounted with groups of winged angels. In every side-chapel, almost, there is some sculpturing or tomb of interest. Beside the western entrance is a spacious chapel with a cupola or dome which is of great interest, for it is the only place in Spain, or in the world, where is still observed the ritual of the primitive Christian Goths as conducted before Spain accepted the Church of Rome. It was permitted by the Moors, was forbidden under Christian kings, and finally restored by Cardinal Ximenes. It is called the "Mozarabe Chapel," or, in English, the Muz-arabic. A simple altar, lecterns and a mosaic and fresco upon the wall are its only furnishings. "The ritual is very simple and imposing," but "has become a liturgic curiosity which must sooner or later disappear." The Cathedral or its site has the usual history of alternate Mosque and Moslem rites and Cathedral and Christian worship. Upon our second visit some great upper shutters in the peak of the roof were open and a flood of sunshine filled the interior, making the great columns seem like alabaster, and as we strolled around and noted the lovely perspectives, the shadows of columns and arches and the large elevated stained windows, often through marble and gilded screens, it was simply enchanting. Just then, we found the Treasury was to be opened for a prominent Spanish statesman and family. It was quite a "function," for six canons in full robes stood in a row, each holding a key. An official took one after another, unlocked a lock and returned it. Five opened the outer gate and one the inner door. The front-

Toledo, Cloister San Juan de los Reyes.

als and robes were superb, some being loaded with coral, and others magnificently embroidered with silver and studded with pearls and brilliants. There were also jewelled paraphernalia, silver statuettes, golden vessels, exquisite crosses and ornaments glittering with gems, and in the centre of the room a tall, cunningly-wrought, gilded temple surmounted by a cross made of gold brought from America by Christopher Columbus. It was not very satisfactory, for the plate-glass doors of the cases were not opened, and the custodian showed the whole display with the light of a candle stump two or three inches in length!

Upon a terrace, overlooking a most striking view of the gorge or ravine made by the river, and of some old ruins and a fine ancient bridge with tower at either end, and far away to the distant mountains, stands the Church of San Juan de los Reyes, a fine specimen of Spanish floriated Gothic, upon one façade of which hang, high upon the walls, the great iron manacles and chains of Christian prisoners liberated after the conquest of the Moors. The interior is fine, being one long aisle with vaults and side walls profusely decorated with arms of Spain, and in a cornice, or covering, a deeply indented text. Adjoining are the famous cloisters, always seen in pictures as more or less ruined and covered with ivy and vines. But as they are now in process of restoration there is no look or suggestion of age. They are magnificent, and surround a square court, are in rich Gothic style, two stories in height, with a wealth of pinnacles. The interior is most profusely decorated with sculpturings of fruit, flowers, heads, leaves and animals, making an exquisite picture as the sun strikes the open arches or floods the parterre of flowers which fills the court.

Adjacent is the church of San Maria de la Blanca, a building which has in its time been a synagogue, stables, warehouse and a Christian church; and now that its working days are done is held and cared for by a society for the preservation of old landmarks. To reach it we passed from the street into a little garden and then into an interior so exquisite and chaste we all exclaimed with delight. A space of eighty-one feet by sixty-three is divided into five naves, an effect reminding in a small way of the Mosque at Cordova. There are thirty-two octagonal columns with Moorish or Byzantine capitals supporting horseshoe arches; and above, a lovely Moorish frieze and an elaborate ceiling of wood,

—a very dreamy and picturesque effect. Then we walked to San Cristo de la Lux, the little ancient Moorish Mosque only twenty-two feet square, with four circular columns supporting sixteen Moorish arches and five half domes,— interesting as being the place where the horse of the "Cid" stopped and knelt, and the wall opened displaying an image of Christ in a niche lighted up by the very lamps the Gothic Christians used centuries before!

The Alcazar looms up so formidably and massively from the hightest elevation in the town, that one little dreams that it is a mere shell—a fire in 1886 having gutted it—leaving only the ponderous and stately outer walls and the magnificent court. This ancient palace of Spanish sovereigns has had a checkered history, beginning in the fifteenth century as a palace, being burned and despoiled in various wars, turned into a silk factory for employment of paupers, into a barracks by the French, and now into a government military school when restorations are complete. From the terrace in front the view is very fine, looking directly beneath upon the pretty, terraced gardens of the town, off upon a ruined castle or two, and farther on along the course of the sinuous, yellow Tagus bending to and fro across the verdant plain, and far away to the billowy horizon hills.

We could not, of course, leave the city without seeing a "Toledo Blade," and where they are made—the royal manufactory—about a mile away. This gave us not only an interesting drive, but a fine view of the old walled city perched upon the rocks. The manufactory is an immense one-storey structure where all the arms of Spain are made. At that time the whole plant was engaged in the manufacture of some newly patented German bayonet. In one room we were shown some genuine Toledo blades and what could be done with them. With incredible and perfect ease these beautiful, glittering swords were bent in shape of a letter S, or twisted and turned in socket-like cases, until one wondered if it could be *steel* so easily handled. In other rooms we saw the delicate and beautiful inlaying of steel with beaten gold. The view of Toledo from the gateway of the works is also fine, for it does not look like a ruined or impoverished town as, high above the irregular Moorish walls, stand, proud and regal, the olden buildings, burnished with golden sunshine. We returned by the bridge of St. Martin which, with arches and towers, spans, high in air, the gorge of the Tagus. The views from it, and from every point, were so picturesque that we laughingly declared "the last is the best." What wonder, as we reluctantly turned away from the majestic and exalted, historical and picturesque city, with the memory of Edinburgh and its gray castle upon the heights, of Perugia lifted high above the billowy surrounding country, of the Kremlin, quaint and palatial, flashing in the sunlight as seen from the Sparrow hills, that we enshrined forever " Toledo, the crown of Spain," perched upon lordly hilltops, with towers and ancient walls and gateways, as we saw it upon those sunny days of opening June?

"THE LARGEST VILLAGE IN SPAIN."

Madrid, as one of the principal capitals of Europe and a centre of much political interest, is well worth a visit, although it is a perpetual disappointment to those who ask for the fish of the national, the typical and characteristic, for it gives them only the stone of the commonplace and the cosmopolitan. One fresh from the old cities, so delightfully and charmingly Spanish, feels at once that the dream is ended, for the long vistas of apartment houses, uniform and monotonous, and the rows of pretty, detached villas with ornamental grounds in the newer portion of the town,—such as are rapidly springing up in the suburbs of almost every European city, from Antwerp to Naples,—are French in character, design and expression. As we entered the spacious and imposing railway station at half-past eight o'clock in the evening, when it was already dark, after a four-hours' journey from Toledo, we really had no "first impressions," for we had seen nothing of the approach to this, the most strangely located city in Europe. The long drive to the hotel along gayly and profusely illuminated streets was most brilliant; but unfortunately we were in little mood for the modern and workaday world and life. When settled we found ourselves facing the oft-quoted "Puerto del Sol," which, however, is not, as its name intimates, a gate of the Sun, but a large open plaza, with a central fountain, modern French buildings, a great crowd of people, and apparently all the street cars in the city. For a place of such magnitude and importance there are but few sights beyond the city itself, but the Royal Picture Gallery, a low, extensive, but imposing structure, with surrounding of lovely gardens, houses a collection of immortal works, which alone are sufficient to make Madrid a shrine to which art lovers and connoisseurs for all time will continually resort. The collection is especially rich in fine specimens of the highest and best period of Spanish art, affording opportunity for study as well as simple enjoyment, since each artist is represented by a large number of canvases. Just think of sixty-four paintings by Velasquez (seen nowhere else to such advantage), forty-six by Murillo, forty-three by Titian, ten by Raphael, sixty-two by Rubens, and large numbers of Tintorettos, Paul

Veronese, Teniers and the celebrated of all lands, under one roof, and some idea will be gained of this peerless, and magnificent array, considered by art critics the finest in the world. Perhaps it is well, as in other celebrated galleries, to gather the *gems* in two beautiful rooms, yet remembering the educational effect of the grouping of the works of Murillo in the Hermitage at St. Petersburg, one could wish that those of each artist here could be seen together. Because of this the feeling at first is of disappointment, for the pictures are so scattered one is easily confused. The Murillos are most enjoyable, although to us none compared favorably with the three marvellous creations at Seville. There are two large Immaculate Conceptions that are wonderful in coloring and expression. One is considered by many authorities as superior to that in the Louvre. While very beautiful it lacks the dreamy, mystical characteristics of the latter. The lovely face is innocence itself, the slight wonder in the eyes marvellous, and the expression of perfect surrender of "do with me as Thou wilt" very fascinating. The atmosphere is peculiarly, deliciously soft and mellow and suffused with gold. As usual, in the tender yellow sheen appear dimly entrancing faces of cherubs. Those below, holding the lily, rose, palm and olive, are in grace of form and attitude and soft delicacy of color simply exquisite. The blue drapery of the Virgin seems floating in the air. It ceases to be paint as you gaze at it; it becomes *color* just as we see it in a rainbow, trembling and seeming as if at any moment it might dissolve or fade away. Near by hangs the other, narrower, but of about same size, in which the cherubs are more beautiful, but the head of the Virgin is thrown back and the roll of the eyes give it an artificial and theatrical appearance. In another room hangs a small and most fascinating picture, "Los Ninos de la Concha," the children of the shell, in which the Infant Christ is giving the child St. John a drink from a scollop shell. A background of verdure throws these two dear little plump figures out in a most life-like way, while the color is dreamy and soft, the fascinating peculiarity of his last, or "vaporoso," style. Close by is another "Immaculate Conception" by him, showing only about one-half of the figure and a large crescent and an earnest, wondering face, which holds one as by a spell. Murillo's Madonnas all have the same face—that of a Spanish peasant—with draperies of rich red and blue. His child faces are simply those of infantile innocence, without any suggestion of mystical Divinity showing through them. This is particularly so in the celebrated "Pajarito," or Holy Family, in which the child holds up a little bird in play with a dog. The child face is exquisite, but it is only a child of the country. They all, for spirituality, compare unfavorably with either the " San Sisto " or the " Seggiola " of Raphael. One cannot pass even a couple of days within the charmed enclosure of these gallery walls without being deeply impressed and enthralled with the strength and power in the pictures of Valasquez, to be studied here as nowhere else in the world. He was probably the greatest portrait painter the world ever saw. His faces are marvellous, and when he puts motion in the figures it is *there*, and you feel the figures will be out of sight in less than no time. There is a portrait, " Prince Baltasar," a boy mounted upon a pony coming towards you, before which you instinctively stand aside lest he run you down! The drapery fairly floats in the air and the pony seems springing from the frame. By him also, in the " Forge of Vulcan," tremendous in drawing. His "Topers " really escapes coarseness and vulgarity by its wonderful expression and coloring. The much praised portrait of Philip IV. we did not seem to grasp, save the horse, which is remarkable. Titian's Charles V. on horseback is called the finest equestrian portrait in the world, surpassing that of Philip IV. of Valasquez. It had been taken to a basement room to be copied for the Austrian Ambassador, but we succeeded in seeing it. The face, pale and ill, is wonderfully determined in expression, but we wondered if we would have suspected it was the finest in the world! Raphael's "El Pasmo de Sicilia" was disappointing in that the faces were like terra cotta in tint and hardness, although the expression of them, the beauty of the figures and the gracefulness of their attitudes, were delightful. His "Madonna of the Fish" is lovely; his "la Perla" very dark and heavy; his "la Rosa" a very charming and graceful grouping, and his "Madonna of the Lizard" beautiful and fascinating, yet none have the sublime power of the peerless San Sisto. The Rubens' are, of course, gross and overfed in figure, but with his irresistibly delightful rose-leaf flesh tints and colors. The Van Dycks are very fine, One room is filled with the works of Goya, a Spanish master not often met. One, a study for a family group, of a Queen in a lace robe, is a marvellous picturing of airy, transparent black lace. The whole collection, in fact, is so fine and numerous that a brief visit is hopelessly bewildering. In the Academy of San Fernando hang three large and superb Murillos, alone worthy the journey to Madrid. All were carried to Paris as spoils of war, but returned to Madrid instead of Seville from whence they were taken. One, a very large and semi-circular canvas, is called "The Dream." Nothing could be more simple in composition or more exquisite in dreamy color. A man sits in a chair, leaning upon a table to one side, asleep. Even the hang of his flesh and the roll of eyeballs betoken profound slumber. Near by, sitting upon a low seat, is a woman with lips slightly parted, and at her feet a tiny pet dog, also asleep. It represents the dream of the Roman patrician which resulted in the building of St. Maggiore in Rome. In the air appears the lovely Virgin and child, and to one side, through an opening, the miraculous fall of snow. The dull reds and blues of the sleepers and the soft white and blue of the Virgin group are delightfully delicate and pleasing. The expression of the whole picture is that of the perfect abandon of sleep. The three forms *sleep*, the man so thoughtfully, the woman so peacefully, and the little dog, animal-like, just *sleeps* and nothing more. Opposite hangs the companion picture, in which the same couple are telling the dream to the Pope. It would be finer, if the other dear charmer was away. Both hung originally in Santa Maria la Blanca in Seville. In the same room hangs his celebrated St. Elizabeth of Hungary feeding the lepers, taken from the Hospital de la Caridad in Seville. It is a most powerful work, a strange mixture of the beautiful and repulsive.

Second only to the galleries in interest is the "Armory," a long, fine room, upon the open plaza of the palace, in which are crowded most superb arms, suits of armor, banners, military trappings, historical curios and jewels and many mementoes of Spain's royal and heroic dead, not the least interesting being the suit worn by Queen Isabella at the siege of Granada. The royal palace is simply enormous, forming a square building some four hundred and seventy-one feet on every side, and walls a hundred feet in height, most peculiarly located upon the edge of a steep ravine. The court being in residence, only the chapel royal could be seen—a great, gaudily and vulgarly gilded and decorated room, with a private box on one side for the family. The view of the distant Guadarrama mountains, icy and cold with perpetual snows, is very fine.

The one outlook at Madrid which charmed us most was that from a terrace or loggia opening upon the great, gravelled plaza to the north of the palace. At this time of the year the verdancy was exquisite, directly beneath us a ravine with numerous trees, everywhere bare, undulating country, a billowy expanse of emerald; and far away in the soft haze of distance the soft pearly and opalescent crests of mountain heights. The situation of Madrid in the midst of bare and desolate hills is most peculiar and unattractive and is accounted for by the fact that Charles V. was a martyr to the gout and found relief in its singularly contradictory climate. Although, some twenty-four hundred feet above the sea level, it is said to be insufferably hot in summer and intolerably cold in winter. A Spanish writer has said, "The air of Madrid is subtle. It kills a man and does not put out a candle."

The day after our arrival was the Sabbath! The windows of the hotel overlooked the principal thoroughfare opening from the Puerto del Sol. In the early part of the afternoon the narrow way was thronged with a crowd of handsome carriages, vehicles of all descriptions and pedestrians passing out of the city toward the

Bull Ring like a great receding wave. Late in the day it all flowed back again like a tidal wave. A momentary touch of color and brilliancy was imparted to the scene by the gayly-attired Picadors upon horseback, and in an open carriage four Matadors gorgeously dressed in rich-colored costumes, resplendent with a profusion of silver lace, embroidery and spangles. They were very merry and laughed and chatted as gayly as if poor Espartero, the second best Matador in the land, had not passed along that way just one week before as confident and unconcerned to come not back again, for he was carried dead from the Ring in the sight of thousands, literally butchered to make a Spanish holiday! But we saw them all return, and word was passed along that it had been a very tame affair, since the Picadors did not even lose a horse! Perhaps it is hardly fair to sweepingly condemn that which one has not seen, but from the reports of fellow-tourists it is impossible to comprehend how this familiarity with constant risk of human life, and this brutal mutilation and cruel death of dumb animals, can be otherwise than demoralizing and deadening to the finer and nobler sensibilities of the individual. But how a custom, inwrought with the religious pageants and fêtes of the present church and the usages of generations, is to be banished, is a problem of the future; for at present there is little or no disposition to attack it.

Earlier in the day, in an upper chamber, we listened for a half hour to the service in the Spanish Protestant church. All along our route we had been much interested in what our friend, long a resident of the country, told us of the night, of the Missions here and there—bright Evangels let us hope of a coming day. There were perhaps one hundred and fifty adults present, and about one hundred scholars. Although we understood not a word, we knew when the Creed was fervently recited and the Lord's Prayer reverently repeated. In their faces was something living, vital and satisfying we had not seen in any Cathedral throng. We wondered if this was not the little leaven which, in the Master's own good time, will leaven the whole lump,—a portion of the unfolding of the heavenly peace on earth, good will toward men, that is certain some day to make the waste places of this goodly land glad!

"THE EIGHTH WONDER OF THE WORLD."

With scarcely a regret, but with an ever-haunting remembrance of the lovely pictures, we turned away from Madrid, and in one hour and a half, owing to the high rate of speed upon the Spanish railways, stood in the shadow of that huge enigma of combined palace, monastery, church and tomb known as "the Escorial," some thirty miles distant from the metropolis. Had it been autumn or winter the intervening country would have been, probably, cheerless and desolate. But as much of it was verdant with turf or golden with ripening grain, the wild flowers, in red, blue, yellow and purple, so profuse and abundant, the great, white, single roses and the yellow gorse so frequent, we thought it really charming. The blood-red poppies never ceased to excite our wonder and admiration, because of the extent or space they often covered, as with a scarlet cloth. The strangest feature was the absence of trees. The soil looked gray and yellow, and very poor, and along the railway is tilled and worked for all, and more, than it is worth. For awhile after leaving Madrid, we had lovely views of the opalescent and amethystine snow-crested range of the Sierra Guadarramas, slumbering mistily and phantom-like in the sunshine. A smart drive up the hill from the station brought us to a comfortable little hotel close to the colossal group of buildings which constitute the famous "Escorial." Every account we had read of it had given us a picture of desolation, barrenness and gloom, so that our first impression of it upon that lovely June day, when the tawny walls seemed to hold and fairly glow with the sunshine, was an unusually cheerful one. It not only, however, overwhelms and dominates with its "bigness," but it dwarfs all surrounding structures into pettiness and littleness. The great, gray bounding hills alone seem of a piece and in harmony with it! This huge extensive building at the foot of bare and desolate hills, with a fussy little village hugging it, with surrounding of bleak, weird and strange landscape, seems out of tune, and like a nightmare, rather than an outgrowth of human life. But that day the walls were so suffused, the neighboring hills so like glistening green bronze, and the town gardens so fresh and fair, that the exterior, at least, lost much of its sombreness, coldness and gloom. Yet it is all very morbid rather than healthful in inspiration and expression. The first view as we approached from the hotel was of the south façade, which appeared like a huge barrack, being a long monotonous structure with pitched roof and dormers. The huge pile forms an outer parallelogram of seven hundred and forty-four by five hundred and eighty feet, and the plan follows the lines of a gridiron in honor of St. Lawrence. Within the outer enclosure of lofty, ponderous, four-storey buildings, are some ten courts, but one only—that of the Monastery, with a central temple and surrounding garden—possesses any beauty. As is well known, the group comprises a monastery, palace and church, all upon a scale of unusual immensity. We entered at the grand portal on the west front, which is directly opposite the central entrance to the church, upon the other side of an immense open court, the Court of the Kings. We were told that at the funeral obsequies of the late king the body laid in state surrounded by royal pomp and heraldic emblazonings in this vestibule, while the spacious court, richly hung in black, was filled with dignitaries in uniforms, listening to the funeral Mass said in a tiny chapel of peculiar sanctity, immediately over the central doorway of the portico to the church. Anything more mournful or sombre can hardly be pictured. Crossing the court we entered the immense sanctuary, said to be the fourth largest in size in the world, and instinctively paused, overawed by the grandeur of its simplicity, the sublimity of its vastness and the solemnity of its sombreness. All is granite, cold, gray, unsculptured granite, unrelieved by color or gold save at the far eastern or high altar end, where both blaze in lavish richness combined with sumptuous colored marbles. There is an awful loneliness, a stern dearth of sympathy and an absolute lack of pitifulness in its expression, in fact nothing one looks and yearns for in the holy temple of the Most High. It does not suggest the soul bowing in glad recognition and grateful worship before its Maker, but rather, shorn of its self-righteousness and filled with morbid despair, lying discouraged because it can offer no price. Not a soul was in the vast structure but ourselves; not a sound broke the awful stillness and oppressive solitariness but our own footfalls. The flickering taper in pendant lamp before the high altar alone suggested hope, for it told of priceless sacrifice and holy presence. Yet in the multitude of long simple lines, the cross-like form and the stately, mighty dome, it is wonderfully fine and impressive, although deadly chill and cold. Standing there, one could not help comparing it with all the color and the dome filled with saints and prophets in St. Peter's, the solemn arches and vistas of St. Paul's and the gold and sheen amid the darkness of St. Isaac's, and feel that this was hard, dry and cold. The high altar is approached by magnificent steps of polished chocolate marble. Above the altar of costly marbles and glittering jasper, rises a very fine and rich retablo some ninety-three feet in height, a sort of reredos, of storey after storey with cornices and columns and spaces or panels filled with paintings, the details of which we could not distinguish in the gloom. Upon either side are doors opening into rooms—royal oratories—above which are open galleries with massive columns and strange, kneeling, gilt, bronze and colored effigies of Charles V. and Philip II. and their families. Numerous chapels open from sides of the church, but they were very dark and of little interest, save one which is the temporary resting-place of the young Queen Mercedes, the first wife of the late king. In the hall-like sacristy we saw the antique and wonderful embroideries which were sent with other historical relics to our Columbian exhibition. Once, this was very rich in sacred vessels, as is proven by the French taking away sixty loads of silver vessels and ornaments. Even now it possesses a small Custodia or receptacle for the Host, fashioned of gold and precious stones, valued at twenty-five thousand dollars. Then we passed down a heavy staircase of stone and came to a portal of richest marble and golden bronze, the entrance to the Royal crypt. The side walls, staircases and round arched ceilings were of polished marbles of various kinds and tints. Perhaps one half of the way down appears upon either side a door. The attendant, with that perfect straightforwardness, inseparable from their routine, announced "these are the rotting rooms!" In other words, the bodies of the Royal family are deposited here for ten years until entirely decomposed, and then the remains of the kings, and such of the queens as have been mothers of kings, are laid in the costly marble sarcophaghi in the crypt, while the remains of all others are taken to a superb suite of burial apartments in another portion of the building. At the foot of the staircase is entered the Royal crypt, a large, octagonal, domed room, some forty-six feet in diameter, directly under the high altar of the church, so that Mass can be said over the

"THE EIGHTH WONDER OF THE WORLD." 193

remains of the kings, every day. Most writers speak of it as cold, gloomy and repulsive. But as it was a glorious sunny day the strange, sumptuous and sombre apartment was full of light and upon every side glittered the richest polished marbles and jasper and gorgeous but vulgar ornamentations of gilded bronze. All around, one above another are deep niches or alcoves, in which lie at full length superb sarcopaghi of gray polished marble with bronze or gilded feet and plates. There were twenty-six or eight of them and only seven occupied. The effect is peculiar and displeasing, but the richness and magnificence of the details could not well be increased, although the taste of it could be improved. The lesser lights of royalty are cared for in a suite of nine or ten rooms superbly floored, walled and ceiled in white marble, wherein are costly tombs, with garniture of gold and enrichments of colored stones, sculptured effigies and adornments, all so clean, fresh and pure, that flooded with sunshine, the effect was very beautiful. But like the whole structure it was bitter cold, and we passed through it all with our warmest wraps closely buttoned to our throats. Up into the gigantic and massive church again and to the Choir, a gallery over the main entrance, but really an immense room with rich stalls of wood, a huge lectern, with enormous books and quaint chandelier of glass, with encircling peacocks, and way off in one corner the stall of Philip II., which could be quietly entered from an adjoining room, the very spot where he was kneeling when a messenger announced the victory of Lepanto. It is said he received the terrible news with unchanged countenance and resumed his prayers. We were glad, after visiting the tiny chapel over the grand entrance (decorated with a large crucifix by Benvenuto Cellini), where the funeral Mass was said for Alfonso XII., to get into the sunshine again. Later we passed through the rooms of the Palace, now shown to visitors, a long suite made unusually bright and cheerful by Spanish tapestries, after Goya, Teniers and others, and draperies of silk and satin, and much charming furniture and a great multitude of old-fashioned clocks, a fad of Charles II. and Ferdinand VII. Then we visited the most interesting portion of all, the suite of four or five rooms occupied by Philip II., who called this stupendous structure into existence. They were very small and with low ceilings, plain and desolate to bareness, with the chair he used as a throne and two rests for his lame limb, and the desk at which he sat writing when told of the total destruction of the Armada. It is related that "not a muscle of his face moved." He only said, "I thank God for having given me the means of bearing such a loss without embarrassment and power to fit out another fleet of equal size; a stream can afford to waste some water when its source is not dried up." His sleeping-room was diminutive and windowless, and opening from it was his oratory or chapel, the windows of which look upon the high altar of the great church, where, on Sunday, September 30, 1598, at the age of seventy-two, he died with his face turned towards the effigy of his father and the high altar. The account of his death is horrible. "For fifty-three days he lay, like Herod, consumed by his own vermin, haunted with doubts whether his bloody bigotry, the supposed merit of his life, was not, after all, a damning crime." A visit to the great library was interesting, although its fifty-six thousand volumes were turned so that the cut gilded edges were to the front, and its gaudy, meretricious ceiling was sadly marred by roof leakage. We missed the pictures in the monastery, owing to an error of our guide as to the hour of closing. This fellow was quite a character, blandly remarking when we engaged him that our "thanks would be sufficient recompense, although his usual price was ten pesetas a day!" We walked in the cloisters and looked in upon the great court of the Evangelists with its temple, statues and box borders, and from various eastern windows looked down upon the surrounding terraces, with fish-ponds and English elms and heavy box borders in stiff geometrical lines and patterns, with not a leaf or flower, but all as gaunt and cold as the great pile itself. Then we gladly went out of this embodiment of man's coldness and morbidness into God's glowing sunlight, and taking a carriage drove back of the town by orchards of oaks and through green fields to the foot of a distant hill and walked to a rocky height where, carved in the rock, is the seat so often occupied by Philip, while watching the slow building of the Escorial a mile and a half away. It commanded a sweeping view of the bare and lonely hills, the mighty architectural pile and the weird, strange country, a billowy stretch of green to the horizon, while, way off in the distance, in the blue haze, like a mirage, trembled the white-crested range of the Sierra Guadarramas. Sitting upon this lonely height, one in hopeless bewilderment gazes at the great enigmatical pile in the distance, the eighth wonder of the world, erected in twenty years, which so dominates the entire scene as to well-nigh occupy the whole thought. A thank-offering for victories won, a filial provision for regal burial, it is also a "whited sepulchre," a lurid memento of Philip II. of which some one has truthfully said, "The man explains the edifice and the edifice is a picture of the man."

A SPANISH UNIVERSITY TOWN.

When the enthusiastic tourist decides to visit the decaying, interesting, historical cities north of Madrid, unless inured to extreme physical fatigue and strain, indifferent as to accommodations and unaffected by inferior diet, his trouble will begin. For, owing to the infrequency of trains, it seems impossible to visit even one without change of trains, and long waits at forlorn junctions or stations in the still watches of the night, or an arrival ere the breaking of the dawn when it is about as easy to get lodgment at the wretched hotels as to effect an entrance into a beleaguered city. Reluctantly we relinquished several places of interest, simply because we were unequal to the continuous strain. But we could not give up Burgos—and we drew a decided line at Salamanca—with its multiform attractions of Cathedral, old palace with walls adorned with scollop shells, the ancient University and the historic battle-field. So one evening at nine o'clock we took, at Escorial, the "train de luxe," the Paris express, and for four hours whirled through numerous tunnels and across the open country in the darkness, until at one-thirty A. M. we alighted at Medina, a junction or something, where was a waiting-room so dingy, ill-lighted and unsavory, and a café or restaurant with atmosphere so blue and dense with tobacco fumes, that we preferred to pass the time of our sojourning in walking upon the platform in the still night air. At two-thirty o'clock the train that was to bear us on appeared. Of course, every one was fixed for the night and asleep, or pretended to be, so that it was quite a feat to distribute and locate our party of six. The remainder of the night passed without incident save that the air grew bitter cold. Between four and five we reached the station for Salamanca, three-quarters of a mile from the town. To our dismay we learned it was Examination week at the University and that the town was full. We hurried ahead of the "'busses" to the principal hotel of the place, an old palace facing a square. The perfect "sang-froid" with which the official in charge showed us, a party of six, the only unoccupied apartment, a room upon the ground floor, with *one* small window and a *single* bed, the English language is unequal to portraying, a kodak could alone have done it justice! In a small but characteristic hotel in a neighboring street we were at last made fairly comfortable, being in a mood to accept what we could get. What mattered it, for were we not in historic Salamanca? A most interesting city it proved, although literally a pitiful ruin with just enough life to keep going. In the fourteenth century it was a centre of learning and ten thousand students flocked to its college halls, but now scarcely five hundred come to its sacred feasts. The French dealt it a cruel and fatal blow, when, for purposes of military defence they destroyed outlying monasteries, churches and colleges, leaving the fine old city forever crippled. Although melancholy and pathetic in expression, it is altogether so interesting and picturesque, it would be a mistake to pass it by. Everywhere in most graphic and often droll contrast, appear evidences of former wealth and elegance and of present squalor and wretchedness. Upon venerable and stately façades, worn and disfigured by centuries of vicissitudes, will frequently be seen, too high to be injured save by the elements, escutcheons with crest or insignia of some noble family, possibly now extinct, beautifully and boldly sculptured in yellow stone, while the windows reveal them the abodes of the most abject and humble poor.

Again, the most forlorn tenement will often have a portal worthy a palace entrance, and upon roofs of neglected and disintegrating structures above the cornice will be seen a cresting or balustrade carved in stone, often of most grotesque or exquisite design. From our windows we looked upon a corner building opposite, the top storey of which had originally shown a tasty little loggia (now rudely closed and plastered up), with delicate arches and columns with two palm-leaf-shaped lozenges with carven crests united with a coronet and ribbon with legend, all in soft tinted stone, dainty enough to set before a king! One of the finest palaces, now deserted, is the Monterey, a long straight building rising in perfectly plain courses of stone like a fortress in three or four, storeys, the upper one forming an arcade or loggia, a succession of arches facing the street with all its columns and brackets and surrounding architectural ornaments richly carved in a multitude of designs. At either end open and very beautiful square towers rise a storey higher, while along the entire roof line is a tall balustrade like guipure lace sculptured in stone. But the one building which really carried us to Salamanca was the famous "Casa de las Conchas," the house of the shells, an old unoccupied Ducal palace, considered one of the most beautiful edifices in the world. It is very odd, and repetition in these later days would perhaps be perilous, but it is unique and very fascinating, the entire, perfectly smooth and plain façade, pierced here and there with most lovely and ornate windows, being ornamented at regular intervals with massive scollop shells, of sculptured stone. Family escutcheons and crests and superb wrought-iron window screens, exquisite enough for a drawing-room, enhance the strange beauty of it. No photographs give an adequate idea of its extreme beauty and irresistible charm, for the lance-like shadows of the shells are so accentuated as to disfigure and deceive. We could have sat all day, but for the beggars and smells, satisfied to simply *look* at it, for the stone is a most peculiar tint and fairly pulses and glows in the sunlight, and the shadows, so ugly in the photographs, are most bewitching. Architecturally it ranks with the Venetian palaces for unaffected grace and genuine beauty. It encloses a dream of a court, exquisite with arches, columns, great lion heads holding rings with shields, adorned with "Fleur de Lys," odd balustrades like banisters interlaced with willows, crestings resembling guipure lace or passementerie in designs of clustered "Fleur de Lys," gargoyles of grotesque conceit and a stately staircase to the upper loggia. As one stands within and opposite the entrance, the towers and domes of the Jesuit church rise so closely beyond as to seem part of the stately, lonely pile. The play of light and shadow, the throng of beautiful ornament and the utter stillness and dreamy repose make the scene enchanting and lasting in impression. But the magnificent Cathedral dominates, as it should, all other structures, for it stands upon an elevation, and, the north side being quite unobstructed, an unusually fine view is obtained of the whole length of it. With its double aisles, flying buttresses, turrets, transept, façade with statues and niches, windows, lantern dome and tall west tower, all in stone, which in color, runs the gamut of tawny yellow, russet and brown, seeming to hold the golden sunlight in great, sweeping patches, it is sublime and impressive to the last degree. The west front is like a huge piece of embroidery, so covered is it with statues, floriated and Gothic ornaments and brackets and canopies, saints, apostles and the "blessed among women." Such edifices seen, like a mighty floriated pyramid, rising against the sunset sky, or in the golden atmosphere of that hour, are indescribable, so unlike in appearance and expression are they from anything in our own land. Beside this grand temple of the sixteenth century is the old Byzantine Cathedral dating from the twelfth century, reached by a wide staircase from the modern church and also from a lower street, with most quaint and interesting interior, with curious capitals, small dome and little chapels. Attached to it is a cloister with chapels, in one of which the Muz-arabic ritual, which in Toledo is said every day, is observed six times in a year. The interior of the great Cathedral is grand in the upward sweep of the columns and arches and the long, cool, quieting shadows of nave and aisles, but disfigured or dwarfed as are many of the Spanish cathedrals, with the choir, a structure of itself, occupying the centre. A most unusual feature are beautiful little Renaissance galleries or balconies in the transepts, and sculptured busts or heads projecting from golden circles, while high above is a most elaborately decorated Gothic roof. Back of the high altar is a necklace of chapels, and somewhere in the edifice is the crucifix which "the Cid" always carried before him in the perpetual conflicts which make the warp of Spanish history, but we failed to see it. In our weariness, our greatest pleasure was in just sitting quietly at the intersection of nave and transept and looking in a desultory way at the general effects, the forest of columns, the touch of color here and there of stained glass, the play of sunlight and shadow and the kneeling figures in black and Spanish mantillas and provincial costumes. Altogether, whether seen from adjacent city streets or from verdant, distant meadows, the antiquated, picturesque pile was to us a joy and delight, and alone recompensed for all the inconvenience of reaching Salamanca.

The ancient University has a marvellous façade and portal, facing a small square, fairly embossed and embroidered with the most refined and delicate carvings of leaves, flowers, etc., in yellow stone, which shows no sign of disintegration or decay. The great buildings enclose a court, architecturally very fine, with arcades and cloisters, and a garden with evergreens, but it suffers much from neglect. We walked through the Library, a noble apartment with groined ceiling and fittings of light wood, and several of the class rooms, some of which were of much historical and personal interest, with the rude forms or desks used in the day of the founder. A little ways from the Cathedral is the church and convent of San Esteban, or Domingo, to which Columbus retired while working out his theory. The front of the church is like a curtain or drapery of most exquisitely and delicately carved stone and does not seem like a building. The interior is fine and impressive with groined roof and the most gorgeous of retablos and altars, all of burnished gilt. The only sign of life was an old monk at prayer in the chancel, and, in little wrought-iron balconies way up on the side wall, two of the brotherhood upon their knees. An English resident friend accompanied us upon a charming stroll to the old bridge, many of whose arches and piers are of Roman construction, and to the high ground without the city. As we looked off upon the surrounding country, a stretch of unbroken and living green, the sunlight, breaking through a rift, threw in prominence a knoll or gentle hill, which was the objective point in the famous battle in 1812 which terminated in the annihilating defeat of the French. As our friend pointed out the position of Wellington, the location of the Scotch troops and the point held by the French, the scene was so peaceful, sunny and prosperous, that it seemed a fabrication. Our Sabbath sojourn was given a familiar tone by attendance at the service in a new, attractive Protestant chapel recently erected by an English society. Freedom of worship and congregating is now permitted by the government (a long stride forward), but in no particular are the buildings allowed to appear like churches. We were much interested in the absorbed attention and reverential mien of the people, who like the Scotch sat with their Bibles open, verifying each allusion and also sang with much spirit. The last hymn, in Spanish of course, was "Jesus paid it all," which appealed very tenderly to us, not, alas! because of any fresh realization of the preciousness and perfection of His glorious redemption, but because it annihilated time and space. Salamanca and its noble structures, Spain and its sunny memories, faded out of mind, and, for the time being, at least, we were in spirit in a dear old and far-away home, with some long in the heavenly kingdom, listening, while a little brown, curly-haired boy sang with childish simplicity and sweetness the same old story and its ever-satisfying refrain.

THE CITY OF THE CID.

There was no choice. We could only leave Salamanca at ten p. m., wait, as before, an hour or so in the midnight air at Medina, where Isabella died, and speed northward with the Paris express. In the "wee sma' hours" we passed Valladolid, where Cervantes lived and Columbus died and thousands of Torquemada's heretics were roasted alive. The assurance of our friend that there was little there but memories and suggestions, and the bright assertion of a popular authoress that the day she spent there was most satisfactory, in that she was satisfied that she never wished to go there again, did much to reconcile us to passing it by. About five-thirty a. m. we left the train at Burgos, the birthplace of the Cid and the final resting-place of his bones, and the situation of one of the most magnificent Cathedrals in Spain. The sky was clear, the air fresh and cool, the streets still and deserted, and the glimpses of long avenues or shady walks and pretty public gardens and statues, prolonged rows of modern houses, the quaint, beautiful, old gateway and the openwork spires of the Cathedral peering above the city roofs, as we drove across a little river, toward and into the town, were a delightful surprise. Such a time as we had effecting an entrance into the hotel, the "Fonda del Norte." The porter was asleep, the door apparently locked and barricaded. They gave us comfortable rooms, but the least said about the rest the better. But we did not expect to live in Burgos on bread alone. We were there *to see*, and we may well cheerfully endure three or four wretched meals, to have come into mind and memory the fadeless picture of the Cathedral alone. The magnificent structure, though, is a jewel upon a rubbish heap, a lily upon the surface of a noisome pool. So crowded is it by mean and common buildings which jostle and fairly stick to it, that although it occupies an elevated position it is seen only piecemeal. It is a pity; for in many respects it is the most airy, ornate and beautiful of all the Spanish Cathedrals. The front or west façade, in color a soiled or grayish white, is fine, with its portals, sculpturings, rose window, balustrade or balcony formed of huge church letters, "Pulchra es et decora," some seventy-three statues of evangelists and saints and two exquisite spires like guipure lace or passementerie, springing gracefully into the blue air some three hundred feet. At the end of a deep court open to the street is seen the south façade also very elaborate, with windows of beautiful design, sculpturings without number and a multitude of statues. As we entered and looked the length of the transept, and a moment later stood at the intersection of the transept and nave and caught the effect of the elaborately ornamented piers, the rich stained glass, the exquisite wrought-iron grilles and the interior of the great dome, covered, as if embroidered, with delicate carvings and tiny balustrades, it seemed as if no general effect could be more lovely. But the longer one looks, the more is he impressed with the lack of meaning in all this profuse decoration. It looks like a garment which is rich and handsome in itself, but is overloaded with sumptuous and incongruous trimmings because the owner happened to have them. It is none the less picturesque, however. As one stands at the west portal, the magnificent structure, following the groined roof, stretches away more than three hundred feet. The great vast nave is airy, and graceful, the aisles upon either side lower but none the less beautiful, and the separating col-

Burgos Cathedl, The Nave.

umns firm and light. It also seems so white and light compared with the interiors of southern Spain. At the intersection of transept and nave springs away in air, with almost a soaring, floating movement, the dome or lantern, profusely decorated with escutcheons and modelled ornaments, till it seems as if decoration could do no more. It is a good example of a style much seen in Spain, called the "Plateresque," which seems to consist in applying or sticking on to the surface, without meaning or expression, any odds or ends of beautiful ornaments one may chance to have on hand.

Following the side of the aisles and around the apsidal end are chapels rich in superb sculptured tombs covered with gorgeous colored velvet palls embroidered with crests, elaborately carved, and gilded altar pieces and retablos, much gaudy decoration and a few good pictures. Back of the high Altar is the Constable Chapel, a church of itself, with a superb lantern dome quite rivalling that of the Cathedral, the property of a noble family who faithfully care for it. The most interesting feature of it is a tomb before the High Altar, which is magnificent, consisting of a rich base or catafalque of polished chocolate-colored jasper, upon which recline two recumbent effigies of Carrara marble, which, yellowed by age, has the appearance of wax. The armor of the man and the flowing robes of the woman are most delicately and elaborately chiselled even to minutest particular. The heads rest upon pillows of marble, which are so delicately ornamented as to look like embroidery or damask. Fine cloisters also connect with the Cathedral, and with their long vistas, sunlit enclosures and cool shadows, are always a picture and delight. The last half hour before leaving the city we passed looking through the grilles and arches, and up to the lantern with the lovely light filtering through the stained windows like a " Shekinah " above and around the high altar. It was a Feast day and they were having a great time carrying around upon a silver covered and draped catafalque, a beautiful, metal cabinet with glass sides, in which, upon satin cushions, rested an old *thigh bone*. The procession as it moved down the dim aisles was extremely picturesque, because of the white and golden robes and draperies of some thirty priests and attendants, with banners and a queer, unfamiliar musical instrument. Meanwhile the music of the organs was very lovely. Later the space before the high altar, filled with kneeling figures in black, flooded with the soft light from above, was most solemn and impressive. Vast in enclosure, beautiful in many details and lavish in ornamentation, it forms a succsssion of exquisite pictures, but, with all, we failed to catch the feeling of Amici when he wrote, "It produces the effect upon you of a superhuman voice which cries, 'I am!'" From the town, a lovely drive of a half hour or more through long shaded alamedas and open country leads to the suppressed Convent of Miraflores, the chapel of which, upon an elevation, with Gothic pinnacles and flying buttresses, looks like an old English rural church and contains the tombs erected by Isabella over the remains of her father and mother, considered prominent among the finest in Europe. Oh! how delicately beautiful they are, although marred by sight-seers and relic-hunters and dingy and discolored by age and neglect. They lie immediately in front of the high altar, and are most wonderfully and elaborately ornamented with sculptured lions, miniature statues, birds, floriated fancies and architectural conceits. But the structures are so tall that the exquisitely wrought effigies, lying at full length upon the top, are not readily or satisfactorily seen. The high altar is interesting, being covered with gold brought by Columbus from America upon his second voyage. A drive of about the same distance in the opposite direction brought us to "Las Huelgas," a convent founded by Eleanor, sister of Richard Cœur de Lion, in which only titled and aristocratic ladies are received or immured by their families. From one side of the uninteresting church, we looked through an immense plate-glass partition upon the superb chapel of the nuns, with costly carved stalls and rich tombs, but the poetical and picturesque white-robed figures at solitary and rapt devotion were nowhere visible and the most romantic feature was wanting.

Although Burgos is the city of the Cid, there is little in the city itself to recall that strange romantic career around which so much historic incident and legendary glamour centre. It was his birthplace, but the home he wished with dying breath to be carried to for burial is some miles away, San Pedro de Cerdena, a Benedictine convent, little of which now remains. Who does not know the chivalric story of the impetuous career for country and for right, the death at faraway Valencia, the ghastly journey home, with funeral pomp, clad in armor, with sword buckled to side, upon his faithful and beloved steed, and his final burial before the high altar of the convent church? In later years the bones of himself and wife were brought to Burgos, where they now have the queerest entombment possible. In the centre of a large salon in the Town Hall (!), a perfect discord of various shades of red, stands a sort of cabinet of dark polished wood which looks like a large work or silver chest and but faintly suggested a sarcophagus. As we entered the room our first thought, as we saw the peculiar creation, was "What is it?" for it is in appearance "neither fish, flesh nor fowl," when lo! it was the veritable tomb of the Cid we had come to see. One's standard of tombs unconsciously gets so elevated in this country that this placing the helpless bones of a hero and heroine in a meaningless workbox in the centre of a commonplace municipal room seems a long step down in character, dignity and respect. The attending senora, in due expectation of a fee, explained to us, that up to a very short time ago, it was never opened save upon great occasions and for distinguishd individuals, but recently the City Fathers had directed it to be shown to any visitor at a certain hour. She turned the key, lifted the hinged cover, and there, under a glass, upon a rich satin cushion, laid a collection of discolored bones. And this was "the Cid" and his faithful wife Ximena! In one corner of the room was an elegant little casket of gold and glass containing some bones of the Cid once spirited away, but returned from Germany with great pomp and ceremony a few years ago. It was not at all impressive and justified the remark of an irreverent bystander, that they were merely " chips from the old block."

BY BISCAY'S SHORE.

FORTUNATELY the enforced and unavoidable night travel, with its attendant loss of all knowledge of the physical aspect of the region traversed, came to an end with Burgos, and we were able to make the journey northward to San Sebastian (eight or nine hours) by daylight, having a most satisfactory view of the varied and pretty Basque country, so unlike in character any other portion of our itinerary. For awhile we seemed in the very heart of a tumultuous stretch of mountains and hills, around, through, over and from point to point of which the railway climbed and curvetted with much of the rollicking defiance peculiar to the Alpine roads. From a high ridge we would look down into depths and upon the road by which we had risen, or forward upon the course before us, while at others we seemed launched upon a billowy sea of hilltops, now dark and sombre with shadows of passing storm-clouds and again flooded with glorious sunshine. Late in the day we came into a district and passed through villages so different from any we had seen that we quite lost our geographical and racial bearing and could have imagined ourselves almost anywhere. About seven o'clock that lovely June evening we entered the handsome station of San Sebastian, the romantic, mediæval and picturesque disappeared, and again we were in conscious touch with the hurrying, progressive life of to-day. As our hotel was a good half mile from the station our drive across the plain and the fine bridge over the river, with glimpses of the sea and farther rocky shores, through avenues of trees and past blocks of fine houses, and finally through the wide, tree-lined street called the "Avenida," gave us a most agreeable first impression of the place. The hotel also was made attractive by surrounding garden, trees and blossoming shrubbery. As it is a seaside resort, in close proximity to the French frontier, it is decidedly cosmopolitan in character and appearance. The long rows of four and five storey buildings with chateau roofs and arcades that mark the business portion, and a majority of the pretty villas that closely stud the shore, are French and not Spanish, while the low, rambling, costly villa of the Queen Regent upon a green knoll overlooking the town and far out upon the blue sea, is so English as to seem like a bit of the beautiful kingdom itself, set temporarily in this dainty scene.

As it was " out of season," the life in the streets was *all* Spanish. The lay of the land is peculiar, the town being built upon a low-lying isthmus formed by the little Urumea wending its way to the seaboard upon one side, and just the loveliest and most picturesque cove or bay imaginable upon the other. If the two were united, a large bay would be formed, and a most beautiful scene obliterated, for the strip, as it reaches the sea, bends and rises into a bold, rocky, tree-embowered hill or height, at the summit of which looms up most picturesquely the walls of an ancient castle. Beyond this, as if already not enough, is a little island. This, in turn, forms the lovely, half-land-locked bay, called "la Concha," the shell, upon which face a showy Casino, hotels, numerous villas stretching along a bathing beach, while the opposite shore is bold, verdant and rock-strewn. It is very lovely—a little Paradise of a watering-place—for there the waves lap softly upon the beautiful bathing beach, and the eye rests upon sunlit waters, bold, rocky shores, picturesque island and castle-crowned heights, and then far away across the waters of Biscay's Bay. A walk to the castle is most fascinating, with exquisite inland and ocean sweeping views. Upon the hillside below the castle is one of the pathetic sights that mark England's course all over the world, a small burial ground with the graves of English officers who followed the Duke of Wellington only to die. The old town has been so tried with fire, having been swept five times, that scarcely anything remains of it. Wellington's troops and blue-jackets, maddened by victory, and probably something else, fired and literally wiped it out. Two old churches remain, and possibly they would have been more interesting had it been the beginning of our tour in a strange land instead of the ending. Costly embankments and quays have been constructed upon the bay where the river debouches, and the boisterous waves of the vicious Bay of Biscay often play sad and destructive havoc upon them. Little San Sabastian has an additional honor in being the capital of a province.

Not the least interesting feature of this pretty resort, to the thoughtful observer, is the cheery Protestant boarding and day school under the care of Mrs. Alice Gordon Gulick and a corps of assistants from our own land, a light in a dark place which cannot but shine more and more unto the perfect day, a refined and Christian home whose influence will be reflected for long years to come in many a Spanish household, through the high intellectual culture and Christian training of its inmates, the future matrons of, let us hope, a new and regenerated Spain. The patient, thorough work which is so admirably carried on is worthy the generous consideration and hearty sympathy of all who care for the Master's Kingdom. Mrs. Gulick, who is a graduate of Mt. Holyoke, was in England under medical treatment at the time of our visit, but the work was most ably cared for. Rev. W. H. Gulick, her husband, has the supervision of all the various mission works in the country, and was the helpful, instructive and charming companion of our whole tour from Gibraltar to San Sebastian.

One afternoon we drove to "Igueldo," a rocky height quite out of sight of San Sabastian. Passing through the groups of fanciful villas which stand along the beach, like a bevy of gayly attired maidens, and beneath the arched passage under the Queen's lawn, and leaving the shore, the road swayed to and fro in its mountings of higher and higher, giving breathless and sweeping views over the hill country and sea-like Biscay. At length we reached a little elevated hamlet, where we left the carriage and climbed the hillside, till we came to the crest which proved to be the topmost rocky ridge like the back of an animal. A rough stone cross gave a strange, weird and lonely expression to it. The magnificent view is so simple and so beautiful, yet most difficult to portray. To our left, like a shoreless sea, the blue waters of treacherous Biscay, as calm and shimmering in the sunlight as if fierce storms were not its normal condition and the rocky shores the scene of many a wreck. It is a rock-bound coast, and as we followed it along, back of us, range after range of hazy purple mountains seemed to move seaward like leviathans coming down to drink. To our right, the hillside dropped hastily and steeply away, and we looked upon a hill-dotted valley, a mass of gentle, bounding, rollicking hills, all fretted into a mosaic of verdant fields and brown fallow lands, while beyond, stretching away to the horizon, shrouded in clouds and darkness, the peaks and rolling, serrated ranges of the Pyrenees. Directly before us, way down in the depths, lay the blue waters of "la Concha," with a faint line of white where the waves broke upon the yellow sands, the long line of chateaux, the Queen Regent's villa and the houses of San Sebastian, in a gray-white semicircle. Way off in the distance a little glimpse of blue waters like a tiny basin in the pretty hill country told of Passages from whence Lafayette sailed to our assistance, and, farther on, a white gleam in the faint coast line marked the location of Biarritz. It seemed so strange to sweep over such a sea as the Bay of Biscay is, and not notice a sail or trail of steamer smoke, but only near the shore a few toy-like fishing-boats. Nothing could surpass the rural beauty of the view to the right. The hills, tickled with the rude ploughs, seem to fairly smile with cultivated fields and orchards, with here and there a red-tiled roof and everwhere the white ribbon-like roads, and in the depths, trees so dense and dark as to be quite forest-like. Another afternoon was most pleasantly whiled away in a visit to Passages, the little seaport, interesting to every American as the one from which Lafayette embarked. A half hour's ride in the tram-car brought us apparently to a little lake or land-locked bay, where were fine new quays and extensive warehouses. But the transformation was complete, for the modern and mediæval were lost in the simple and picturesque. We wondered where we were, it was so dramatic, so like an artificial set scene ! Across the quiet pool a single row of houses crowded and jumbled together, with gables and balconies almost completely covering the fronts, all close to the water's edge. All colors and forms, old churches, the laundry of about every family flying in the breeze from every balcony, ancient fortifications and rough dark hills beyond, seen through air crystalline in clearness, with the reflection in the smooth waters, made a picture of striking quaintness and beauty. Strong, sturdy, bareheaded women rowed the boat across the quiet harbor, and then we walked along the one narrow street scarcely wide enough for a cart and went up to the old fortifications, which commanded a fine view of the very narrow gateway or passage to the sea, and far out upon the turbulent waters. The little town rejoices in the name of " St. John," while the " passage " upon the opposite side of the inlet, a single street with droll houses and sights and an old church, is none the less complacent under the title of " St. Peter." It is little to tell of, but between the old churches with queer belongings, the quaint, arched passageways, the picturesque confusion of gables and corners, the peaceful restful bay and the surrounding sombre and flower-starred hills, and the striking contrast of the almost angry waters of Biscay stretching away to the horizon, we could have tarried there all day as happy as in a dream. Perhaps we ought to have thought and have recalled the never-to-be-forgotten service of Lafayette, but somehow, in the light of altered circumstances, the lapse of years, the exquisite restfulness and "dolce far niente" of that sunny, mellow afternoon, the old thrilling story seemed, and floated in our minds, as some far-away and beautiful poetic myth with which this land so richly abounds.

THE BIRTHPLACE OF A DEVOTEE.

One absolutely perfect day was filled to the overflowing by a charming drive in an easy open carriage to Azpeitia, the birthplace of that grave, gloomy, mysterious character, the founder of the order of Jesuits, Ignatius Loyola. Again we drove along the wave-lapped beach, past the pretty villas, under the Queen Regent's lawn, and leaving the shore turned inland, through a valley or bed between great, bounding hills which reminded us of our own Berkshire county. It was a lovely drive from beginning to end, a constant succession of rural pictures, kaleidoscopic in variety and rapidity of change. Sometimes the way would follow a stream winding and bending between shaded banks, like a pretty English river, and at intervals most picturesque glimpses were had of curving, shaded, walled roads with groups of peasants plodding along, the women carrying their babies upon their backs, or fields with women in dull reds and blues quite suggestive of Murillo's mellow tints. Stone walls along the road, arched bridges of stones and a road as smooth as a park drive, demonstrated the care and thrift of the Province. The first village of any size was decidedly Italian in character, a mixture of Swiss and Italian, rather than Spanish. A fine old palace, with sculptured crest and broad eaves, was quite like those often seen in Italy. Our way then led to and fro along densely wooded hills, the smooth road often doubling upon itself. Some of the very wide, rude houses were fairly covered with grapevines, and often nestling among the trees upon opposite hillside a gable and roof would show, that needed only the stones upon it to make it appear a Swiss chalet. Often the white road could be seen wriggling and bending a long way in front of us. Another dirty Italian-looking village upon a river's bank, with a pretty glimpse of the sea, was passed. Very pretty too were the old stone bridges and the new viaducts of a narrow gauge road in process of construction. Then we climbed slowly a hill, first facing one way and then another, looking down constantly upon the white road traversed. Oh, how gentle, verdant and fresh the country appeared! Suddenly, away before us, appeared the blue waters with a great, emerald, rocky island across the mouth of an inlet. It was like a sudden lifting of a stage curtain, so entirely different was it. Soon we entered a long avenue of Lombardy poplars, stiff and straight, passed iron fences through which we looked at well-ordered grounds and tasteful summer villas, and came to a large and populous town where we rested for a half hour, or rather the horses did, for immediately we sought out the old church, which had showy golden retablos and a pretty, inverted, curved gallery. A road bent off to one side with high walls, overhanging trees and pendant ivy. We were close to the sea, but did not know it until later in the day, when we came again into the little town by this picturesque way. The town had the look of centuries, but—a woman sat by an open window with a sewing-machine, upon the side of which was the magic "Singer!" Then along the lovely country road again! There were no patches of wild flowers, not even the familiar stretch of scarlet poppies. The land is too well cultivated for that. On the road banks great bunches of purple heather were breaking into bloom: hundreds of privet shrubs, suffocating in odor, were white with blossoms, pink and white single roses showed here and there in the hedges, and along the way the dear

THE BIRTHPLACE OF A DEVOTEE.

little Pimpernels were thick as among the tumbled rocks of Maine. We sped along a narrow valley, upon side hill, by a viaduct to opposite slope, until we came into a more open country, the hills becoming bolder, the valleys wider and the general scenery more striking. We seemed no longer in valley depths, but upon hillsides with roads hewn out of them and bold mountain views, fine farms, great red-roofed houses, cloud-tipped distant ranges and beautiful villas ever before us. Down and down, to and fro, our way laid until we reached about midday the village of Azpeitia, a half mile or more beyond which, in a delicious green valley, is situated the "Casa Santa," the monastery and church which environ the birthplace of Ignatius Loyola. It is a huge pile of monotonous buildings with the irregular portico of the church projecting from the centre. To one side is a hotel and in front two lovely shaded walks of horse chestnuts trained upon a trellis. The church is imposing in size, but tawdry, cheap and ugly in effect, abounding in gray marble and stucco-work. In the huge dome appear family crests upon draperied backgrounds, here and there is a touch of gold, and before the side chapels exquisite crystal chandeliers. The men of the party were conducted through the monastery proper by a most agreeable and entertaining "Father," Irish by birth, but Spanish by adoption and long residence. The Library, the plain refectory, the garden, courts, corridors and cells were visited consecutively. They were extensive and commodious, delightfully sweet and clean, but in spite of a wealth of sunshine were all as white and cold as the personal life they extinguish or impoverish. The house in which Loyola was born is incorporated within the monastery walls and is shown to every one, and is in every way disappointing. The outer walls were shown, and in the next breath we were told they were only exact replicas. Then we were taken upstairs where were several low ceiled apartments, the genial guide remarking that the ceilings and floors were the originals, but the partitions had been removed to adapt the rooms to pilgrimages and religious ceremonies. In one room, however, stands unchanged the old altar of the family. In another the identical place is shown where he was laid when sore wounded he was brought home from the siege of Pamplona. As is well known, it was while lying here—in his long convalescence—that his whole life was changed through reading and meditating upon the "Lives of the Saints," etc. But they have spoiled it all by vulgarly ornamenting and elaborately gilding the ceilings in a way utterly foreign to the dramatic and pathetic story. The rooms are arranged with open screen partitions so that the vulgar crowd can kneel and "long to enter in." Standing there and recalling the striking incidents of his career, the religious thought and influence of his time and the cruel, terrible power which even to-day is the outgrowth of his work, one could not help thinking what the result of equal self-renunciation, devotion and consecration, in the clearer shining of this age, might do for the evangelization and salvation of this sin-touched world. Whether one sympathizes with it or not, the story of this life is thrilling and interesting and inspires in a thoughtful mind a very deep and solemn question. The location of the buildings is fine and striking. To the rear, an amphitheatre of hills. In front, a wide, level, fertile valley. To the left, a great sloping mountain covered one-third of the way up with verdure and showing beyond almost entirely bare gray rocks. In front, far away beyond the valley and the village, a great hump or mound-like mountain, gray, grizzled and mottled with green, while to its right a mountain range bounds away as if to tell the world a child was born whose impress would be for succeeding centuries a terrible power upon it.

In far-a-away Rome, by the yellow Tiber, in the church of "Il Gesu," in the transept chapel dedicated to his memory, in an urn of gilt bronze, beneath a gorgeous altar enriched with his statue in silver and a group of the Trinity with a globe of lapis-lazuli, said to be the largest piece in existence, in the midst of all the meretricious magnificence that gold and precious marbles can express, "after life's fitful fever he sleeps well"—but alas! his works do follow him.

Upon our return we followed for awhile the road by which we came and then branched off into a purgatorial, uninteresting country only to emerge upon a paradisaical scene, as for four or five miles we drove along a fine, smooth road cut out from the rock-bound coast, bordered and protected by a handsome parapet or wall. The extreme beauty of this portion of the drive is beyond word-picturing. It consisted in the constant bending and curving along a sharp ragged inhospitable shore, but with no variety of scenery as along the Salerno coast. The views backward were superb, for the mountain ranges were very abrupt and irregular and the great piles in the hazy atmosphere were mellow with amethyst and delicate violet, while the sunlight effects upon the broad waters were marvellous. We were sorry when there was no more road and "no more sea," and we again turned into the little village where, in the morning, we had rested for a half hour. Then back by the same enchanted way of the earlier part of the day with the quiet, solemn shades of evening gathering and thickening with every mile. It was nine o'clock when the horses' hoofs clattered along the quiet streets of San Sebastian and brought us again to our hotel, tired of course, but with one more delicious memory of what has really been to us "sunny Spain."

AU REVOIR.

As the train carried us away from jaunty little San Sebastian, a dreary sense that vacation was ended possessed us, that our romantic, interesting and instructive journey was nearing its close, and that already we had crossed the country of the Little King. Perhaps in the olden days when the only mode of conveyance was the diligence, the common post-coach of the country, and the long desolate stretches were slowly covered, necessitating frequent stoppings at wretched wayside inns and always a possibility of a "hold-up," all that has been written and said about the hardship, fatigue and danger of Spanish travel may have been true. But the advent of the railway has altered all this, and one can see a good portion of the kingdom, in comparative comfort, although, doubtless, at the expense of many a characteristic feature. Yet, neither in road equipment nor in accommodation along the route, will a trip as yet compare in luxury or comfort with any of the great Continental routes. Some one will say (in fact, we have been repeatedly asked) "Does it pay?" To this we answer, "It depends upon the individual!" Any one who cares more for what there is to be seen than for what he must eat, or where he must lodge, will find it yielding a hundredfold. We would gladly have repeated the whole route and only regretted we had not allowed more time and visited more places. But tastes differ! For instance, said a vivacious little western woman, our "vis-à-vis" at table d'hôte at San Sebastian, at the completion of an extensive tour, "There is nothing worth seeing in Spain but the bull-fights, and they are *horrid, horrid!*" Infinitesimal questioning revealed the fact that, although "horrid," she had repeatedly witnessed them! "They are so characteristic, you know! Just what one comes to Spain to see!" While half listening to the ripple of light conversation which followed, our thoughts were busy with the pictures memory holds so dear,—of the majestic leonine form which gave us our first welcome, the quaint cork trees and olive-dotted slopes and verdant stretches of fair and winsome Andalusia, the flowers which garlanded as for a fête our whole route, the marvellous canvasses at Seville and Madrid, the vast stupendous structures which in the Cathedrals of Seville, Toledo, Salamanca and

Burgos, embody the worship of a past age,—the magnificent tombs,—the impress of Roman, French and Moor in the architecture of the various cities,—grand old Toledo, lifted high in air, the peerless Alhambra and the faultless Geralda, and the fascinating and delightful "unlike anything else" of many characteristics of the towns, the interesting people and the pretty Basque country. and said quietly to the national sport, the bull-fight, "To us, you are weighed in the balance and found wanting,"—to *our* taste you form the least satisfactory of all the attractions and characteristics of grand old and half-awakened Spain!

* * * * *

A journey of three-quarters of an hour, past Carlist, tower-crowned hills and through uninteresting country, brought us to "Irun," our last Spanish town. Way off upon the hillside, solitary and alone, was a huge structure with a tower, probably a monastery: beyond in a line of several miles great square towers for watch and defense, a reminiscence of the last great Carlist war, and upon a point jutting out into the little river, the group of buildings and towers comprising the town.

A few moments beyond the stream we came to Hendaye,—and were upon French soil. As we slowly bridged the little river, a fair young girl of the party, in the exuberance and joyousness of youth, tossed lightly into the shining waters a new copper coin—that she, and let us hope,—all of us, might come again to the castles we have builded all our lives long, in romantic, chivalric and poetic Spain,—the treasured country of the Little King.

THE END.